Infant/Toddler Caregiving

A Guide to

Cognitive Development and Learning

Second Edition

Edited by

Peter L. Mangione

Developed collaboratively by the

California Department of Education

and WestEd

with funding from

Carnegie Corporation of New York

  WestEd

Publishing Information

Infant/Toddler Caregiving: A Guide to Cognitive Development and Learning (Second Edition) was developed by WestEd, San Francisco. See the Acknowledgments on page viii for the names of those who made significant contributions to this document. This publication was edited by Faye Ong and John McLean, working in cooperation with Peter Mangione, WestEd, and Lisa Duerr and Sy Dang Nguyen, Consultants, Child Development Division, California Department of Education. It was designed and prepared for printing by the staff of CDE Press, with the cover designed by Juan Sanchez. It was published by the Department of Education, 1430 N Street, Sacramento, CA 95814-5901. It was distributed under the provisions of the Library Distribution Act and *Government Code* Section 11096.

ISBN 978-0-8011-1732-9

Ordering Information

Copies of this publication are available for purchase from the California Department of Education. For prices and ordering information, please visit the Department Web site at http://www.cde.ca.gov/re/pn/rc or call the CDE Press Sales Office at 1-800-995-4099.

Notice

The guidance in *Infant/Toddler Caregiving: A Guide to Cognitive Development and Learning (Second Edition)* is not binding on local educational agencies or other entities. Except for the statutes, regulations, and court decisions that are referenced herein, the document is exemplary, and compliance with it is not mandatory. (See *Education Code* Section 33308.5.)

Prepared for printing
by CSEA members

Contents

iii

A Message from the State Superintendent of Public Instruction

Cognitive development and learning in the early years is interwoven with development and learning in all other domains. Six noted experts have been brought together to create this second edition of the Program for Infant/Toddler Care (PITC) *Guide to Cognitive Development and Learning*. It focuses on discoveries and intellectual development during the early years; the effect of caregivers' responsiveness on early development and learning, brain development, and social interactions during the early months of life; and the role of culture in cognitive development. This publication provides guidance on implementing high-quality early care and education programs.

Special attention has been given to understanding infants and toddlers as active, self-motivated learners who are constantly exploring their relationships with others as well as the physical environment. Just as important as children's active role in early learning is sensitive, responsive nurturance. It fosters development in all domains and contributes to intellectual ability throughout childhood. Children also learn essential cultural practices and become competent participants in their communities. Above all, this resource offers infant/toddler care teachers many practical ideas on how to create relationships with children that encourage exploration and discovery and helps children become confident learners throughout life.

The guidelines and suggestions in this publication complement the research-based descriptions of cognitive development of typically developing young children that appear in the *California Infant/Toddler Learning and Development Foundations*. It is our hope that everyone in the infant/toddler field can use this new publication hand in hand with the other resources created by the Department of Education to promote the well-being and long-term development of California's youngest children and their families.

Tom Torlakson

TOM TORLAKSON
State Superintendent of Public Instruction

About the Authors

Marc H. Bornstein is the editor of *Parenting: Science and Practice* and senior investigator and head of child and family research at the Eunice Kennedy Shriver National Institute of Child Health and Human Development. Bornstein is coauthor of *Development in Infancy* (five editions); *Development: Infancy Through Adolescence; Lifespan Development;* and *Perceiving Similarity and Comprehending Metaphor.* He is general editor of *The Crosscurrents in Contemporary Psychology* series, including *Psychological Development from Infancy; Comparative Methods in Psychology; Psychology and Its Allied Disciplines* (Vols. I–III); *Sensitive Periods in Development; Interaction in Human Development; Cultural Approaches to Parenting; Child Development and Behavioral Pediatrics;* and *Well-Being: Positive Development Across the Life Course.* Bornstein is also general editor of the Monographs in Parenting series, including *Socioeconomic Status, Parenting, and Child Development; Acculturation and Parent–Child Relationships;* and *Parenting: Essential Readings.* He edited *Maternal Responsiveness: Characteristics and Consequences,* the *Handbook of Parenting* (Vols. I–V, two editions), and the *Handbook of Cultural Developmental Science* (Parts 1 and 2). Additionally, Bornstein coedited *Developmental Science: An Advanced Textbook* (six editions), *Stability and Continuity in Mental Development, Contemporary Constructions of the Child, Early Child Development in the French Tradition, The Role of Play in the Development of Thought, Acculturation and Parent–Child Relationships,* and *Immigrant Families in Contemporary Society.* He is author of or consultant on several children's books, videos, and puzzles in *The Child's World and Baby Explorer* series and is editor emeritus of *Child Development.*

J. Ronald Lally is codirector of the WestEd Center for Child and Family Studies, Sausalito, which created the Program for Infant/Toddler Care (PITC) for the California Department of Education. The caregiver training system provides videos, written materials, and technical assistance. Lally is the coauthor, with Ira Gordon, of *Learning Games for Infants and Toddlers;* coauthor with Alice Honig of *Infant Caregiving: A Design for Training;* and coauthor with Kuno Beller, Ira Gordon, and Leon Yarrow of *Studies in Socio-Emotional Development in Infancy.* Dr. Lally also directed the Syracuse University Family Development Research Program, an early intervention program for children (from birth to age five) of low-income families. He is currently directing the longitudinal follow-up study of the effects of the Syracuse program.

Elita Amini Virmani is a senior research associate with the WestEd Center for Child and Family Studies. She is the director of the PITC Home Visiting Institutes, funded by the Early Head Start National Resource Center. She also manages the development of the California Department of Education, Child Development Division's Desired Results

Developmental Profile School Readiness instrument. Elita Amini Virmani served as an instructor at San Francisco State University and West Valley College. She received intensive clinical training at the University of California, San Francisco Infant-Parent Program, where she provided clinical services to low-income, multiethnic families and mental health consultation to child care program staff and parents of children with special needs. She has published articles in the *Infant Mental Health Journal, Early Childhood Research Quarterly, Journal of Psychopathology and Behavioral Assessment,* and the *Handbook of Cultural Developmental Science*.

Tiffany Field is director of the Touch Research Institute (TRI) at the University of Miami Medical School. The TRI was the first center in the world devoted solely to the study of touch and its application in science and medicine. The TRI researchers—a distinguished team representing Duke, Harvard, Maryland, and other universities—strive to better define touch as it promotes health and contributes to the treatment of disease. Research efforts that began in 1982 and continue today have shown that touch therapy has numerous beneficial effects on health and well-being. Dr. Field is a leading researcher and authority on the benefits of touch and has conducted several research studies based on the ancient practices of infant massage from various cultures of the world. Her groundbreaking research indicates that massage therapy used on babies born prematurely increases their healthy weight gain; consequently, they can be discharged much earlier than infants who did not receive nurturing touch through massage therapy.

Lucía Alcalá is a doctoral candidate from the University of California, Santa Cruz (UCSC), as of June 2012. Her research focuses on the cultural variation of children's contributions to family work and participation in out-of-school activities and how those levels of participation influence children's development of planning skills, initiative, and responsibility. Alcalá is currently the editor of the UCSC Department of Psychology newsletter and a teaching associate in the department. She is the recipient of the 2011 Max Levine Scholarship award and numerous other awards in her field.

Barbara Rogoff is UC Santa Cruz Foundation Distinguished Professor of Psychology. She has held the position of University of California Presidential Chair and has been a Fellow of the Center for Advanced Study in the Behavioral Sciences, a Kellogg Fellow, a Spencer Fellow, and an Osher Fellow of the Exploratorium. She served as editor of *Human Development* and of the newsletter of the Society for Research in Child Development, Study Section member for the National Institute of Child Health and Human Development, and committee member on the Science of Learning for the National Academy of Science. Rogoff is the author of several highly regarded books in her field: *Apprenticeship in Thinking* (1990) received the Scribner Award from the American Educational Research Association; *Learning Together: Children and Adults in a School Community* (2004) was a finalist for the Maccoby Award of the American Psychologist Association; and *The Cultural Nature of Human Development* (2003) won the William James Book Award of the American Psychological Association.

Acknowledgments

The first edition of this publication was developed by the WestEd Center for Child and Family Studies, under the direction of J. Ronald Lally. Funding for the first edition was generously provided by the Carnegie Corporation of New York. Special thanks go to Marc H. Bornstein, Helen G. Bornstein, Tiffany Field, Theodore D. Wachs, and Peter L. Mangione for their contributions to the first edition; to Karla Nygaard for editorial assistance; and to Janet Poole and Mary Smithberger, Child Development Division, California Department of Education, for their review of the content. Thanks are also extended to the members of the national and California review panels for their comments and suggestions. The national panel members are T. Berry Brazelton, Laura Dittman, Richard Fiene, Magda Gerber, Asa Hilliard, Alice Honig, Jeree Pawl, Sally Provence, Eleanor Szanton, Yolanda Torres, Bernice Weissbourd, and Donna Wittmer. The California panel members are Dorlene Clayton, Dee Cuney, Ronda Garcia, Jacquelyne Jackson, Lee McKay, Janet Nielsen, Pearlene Reese, Maria Ruiz, June Sale, Patty Siegel, and Lenore Thompson.

For contributions to this second edition, special thanks go to Marc H. Bornstein, J. Ronald Lally, Lucía Alcalá, Barbara Rogoff, Elita Amini Virmani, and Peter L. Mangione. For editorial assistance, appreciation is extended to Eva Gorman.

The California Department of Education gratefully acknowledges Sara Webb Schmitz for the use of photos that appear in this publication. Special thanks go to the following programs: Associated Students Sacramento State University, Children's Center; Blue Skies for Children; the Cameron School; Contra Costa Community College Early Learning Center; Eben Ezer Family Child Care; Little Munchkins Academy; Marin Head Start, Hamilton Campus; Marin Head Start, Indian Valley Campus; Marin Head Start, Meadow Park Campus; and Willow Street Schoolhouse.

Introduction

Studies consistently show that a baby learns most and fastest—and will likelier remember what he learns—when he can control what's happening. . . . it's those experiences he chooses (not necessarily those chosen for him) that help him learn fastest and most completely.

Evelyn B. Thoman and Sue Browder
Born Dancing, pp. 109–110

Experts in early childhood development and care have increasingly recognized the importance of giving infants and toddlers the freedom to initiate and direct their learning. Yet many articles and books urge infant/toddler care teachers to be in charge of the kinds of stimulation that infants and toddlers experience. Teachers have been told to "teach" babies early in life and to do special activities or else the children will likely miss key learning experiences. In addition, countless numbers of educational toys and materials have been designed to teach babies specific lessons. This push to teach and control the experiences of infants and toddlers is balanced by an awareness of the effect of too much stimulation on babies. Indeed, the researchers question the value of teaching infants and toddlers, especially when teaching interferes with children's self-initiated exploration and learning (Gopnik 2009). Thoman and Browder (1988) suggest that in optimal learning situations, babies are in control, yet formal teaching usually takes control away from them.

If being in control is beneficial for babies, what is the teacher's role in early cognitive development and learning? In a nutshell, the teacher plays a special part in the learning and development of an infant or toddler. The teacher's role includes being responsive to the infant, engaging in back-and-forth interaction, offering opportunities for the infant to participate in care routines, setting up the environment, providing interesting and developmentally appropriate equipment and materials, and connecting the infant's cultural and linguistic experiences at home with experiences in the infant/toddler care setting. These topics are among the ones that will be highlighted in this guide. Missing from this list is teaching. The teacher and the infant are usually occupied with far more important matters than the content of a specific lesson. How the naturally occurring actions of infants and toddlers contribute to their early development is the subject of this guide.

Does allowing babies to be in control of their learning mean that teachers should always follow babies' lead or let them play on their own? Or should teachers initiate interaction and try to interest infants in playing together? The answer to these questions is—it depends. Too often the debate on whether to initiate interaction with babies has been reduced to all or nothing. Some experts say that adults should initiate and guide infants' learning; others suggest that following the lead of infants is the most effective way to support their learning. But adults cannot help but initiate interaction and play with babies, even if they try not to do so. In caring for infants and toddlers, infant/toddler care teachers naturally talk, provide guidance, structure the environment, and nurture children. All of these actions stimulate babies directly or create conditions that do so. Infants and toddlers need this initiative from teachers to develop and thrive in group care settings.

However, the matter is more complicated than simply initiating and guiding early learning. For example, when is an infant ready for interaction? Is the adult's verbal and nonverbal communication simple enough for the infant to follow and learn from? Is it interesting to the infant? Is it too loud or too fast? Answers to such questions have to be considered from the perspective of the infant. And for that perspective to be understood, the infant's reactions to stimulation have to be observed. The infant has to be allowed to act and react. Letting the child initiate learning and exploration is the key to (1) understanding his or her interests and reactions; and (2) deciding whether a certain type of response is appropriate or inappropriate.

Giving infants and toddlers opportunities to be in control of their learning and exploration not only benefits their development but also enables the teacher, through observation, to discover appropriate responses and thereby support early cognitive development and learning. Knowing what to look for in the actions of infants and toddlers is helpful. Sometimes the actions of infants may appear unimportant to the casual observer, but the children are learning on their own terms—the best approach available to them. In "Discovery in Infancy: How and What Infants Learn," J. Ronald Lally illuminates how simple actions (for example, sucking on a toy) are profoundly important to infants. With an emphasis on the actions, interests, and needs of infants and toddlers, the chapter gives an overview of development during infancy—in particular, the processes of learning and discovery. The adult's response to an infant's actions, especially when the child expresses a want or need, is also important.

The relationship between responsive caregiving and cognitive development is addressed by Marc Bornstein in "Caregiver Responsiveness and Child Development and Learning: From Theory to Research to Practice." Bornstein defines responsiveness, examines characteristics of responsive caregiving, and summarizes research on the developmental impact of responsive caregiving. He suggests that a major part of being responsive to infants is knowing when to engage in social interaction with them.

Responsive nurturance in a close relationship establishes the foundation for the baby's emotional security and promotes cognitive development. J. Ronald Lally and Elita Amini Virmani, in "Learning During the Early Months," examine the impact of children's early relationship experiences on the developing brain and on children's early emotional and intellectual capacities. They describe how early interaction experiences in relationships shape the brain. In essence, interactions early in life can affect cognitive development and learning positively or negatively. Positive interactions foster secure relationships and strengthen infants' confidence to explore the people and objects in their world.

To make the most out of interactions with infants, caregivers need to modulate their responses to match the children's ever-changing interests, needs, and moods. In "Supporting Cognitive Development Through Interactions with Young Infants," Tiffany Field describes how the level of alertness and activity of infants affects their ability to learn through interactions with an adult. An infant/toddler care teacher who is sensitive to such factors will be better able to engage an infant in increasingly prolonged interactions. Field also suggests how teachers can adapt their behavior to an infant's emerging capacities.

While Section One of this publication focuses on general areas of cognitive development and the role of responsive nurturance in close relationships, Section Two considers the context for early cognitive development and learning. Lucía Alcalá and Barbara Rogoff, in "Culture and Cognitive Development," state, "Infants and young children learn from their day-to-day activities with other people in specific cultural communities that promote practices that are often supported by the members of families and communities." Infants begin to learn repertoires of cultural practices by being immersed and taking part in everyday events and routines. These repertoires lead to the development of a "wide range of cognitive skills." Alcalá and Rogoff recommend that infant/toddler care teachers approach a family's cultural practices with an open mind. In doing so, teachers can help children learn practices outside their home and help them know which practices fit in which setting.

The appendix reprints the cognitive development domain from the *California Infant/Toddler Learning & Development Foundations* (California Department of Education 2009a). There are 10 foundations in the cognitive development domain, such as cause-and-effect, problem solving, number sense, and symbolic play. The research literature that underlies each foundation is summarized. Along with each foundation is a table with descriptions of children's competencies at around eight months, at around 18 months, and at around 36 months. In addition, each table displays a list of behaviors leading up to the foundation for each of the three ages. The foundations are reprinted in this publication so the reader will have available in one resource both recommended practices for supporting early cognitive development and in-depth information on early cognitive development.

Some topics in this guide are covered to the exclusion of others. Two key topics that have received limited treatment are the environment and caregiving routines. The lack of attention given to these topics is not meant in any way to diminish their importance in early cognitive development and learning.

The environment affects infants' and toddlers' cognitive development in manifold ways. Factors such as the lighting, air quality, traffic patterns, noise level, and amount of materials influence children's capacity to maintain attention while exploring and learning. High-quality environments ensure that infants and toddlers can engage in play and interaction without distraction. Such environments offer equipment and materials that are challenging for the age and stage of the children. The indoor and outdoor environments are organized so that children know the purpose of each area; for example, dress-up clothes are in an area with props for pretend play, blocks are located with space for building, and books are available in a quiet area, sheltered from active play. The publication *Infant/Toddler Caregiving: A Guide to Setting Up Environments* (California Department of Education 2009b) addresses these considerations and many more.

Care routines, such as feeding and napping, are central in the care of infants and toddlers. For many reasons, experts say that routines are the curriculum from which infants learn. During routines children learn about their bodies, their needs, their likes, and their dislikes. As they eat, they discover the taste and texture of different foods. If performed in a consistent, organized way, care routines make life predictable for infants and toddlers. Predictability in a child's daily life supports both social–emotional and cognitive development. The child can begin to understand and anticipate order in his or her world.

Throughout this guide, opportunities for one-to-one contact with an adult are cited as important in early development, and routines often give an infant a chance to have one-to-one time with a teacher. The role of routines in early development, including cognitive development, is given in-depth coverage in *Infant/Toddler Caregiving: A Guide to Routines* (California Department of Education 2002).

This guide explores how the natural activities that infants and toddlers naturally engage in contribute to their learning and development. During virtually every waking moment, infants are learning and making discoveries, particularly when they have the freedom to choose the focus of their learning and exploration. Whether banging a rattle on the floor or looking for an object or participating in a routine such as eating, infants are engaged in significant learning. Infants and toddlers benefit greatly when they have a caregiver who is sensitive and responsive to their interests and needs, who creates developmentally appropriate environments, and who encourages them to explore freely and be in control of what happens. The following pages offer many insights and ideas for teachers seeking to provide that kind of support to infants and toddlers.

References

California Department of Education. 2002. *Infant/Toddler Caregiving: A Guide to Routines*. 2nd ed. Sacramento: California Department of Education.

————. 2009a. *California Infant/Toddler Learning & Development Foundations*. Sacramento: California Department of Education.

————. 2009b. *Infant/Toddler Caregiving: A Guide to Setting Up Environments*. 2nd ed. Sacramento: California Department of Education.

Gopnik, A. 2009. *The Philosophical Baby: What Children's Minds Tell Us About Truth, Love, and the Meaning of Life*. New York: Farrar, Straus & Giroux.

Thoman, E. B., and S. Browder. 1988. *Born Dancing: How Intuitive Parents Understand Their Baby's Unspoken Language and Natural Rhythms*. New York: HarperCollins.

Section One:

Cognitive Development
and Learning

Discovery in Infancy: How and What Infants Learn

J. Ronald Lally

Our personhood begins in infancy, a stage rich with activity. An understanding of how young children form lasting relationships, start communicating with others, and bring order to their world can turn your time with the child you care for into an adventure. You see a personality emerging, a mind struggling to make sense of experience. You see the child in the early stages of creating her or his reality—bringing meaning to each event, each action.

With what looks like crude and primitive actions, infants give structure, order, permanence, and predictability to their experiences. Infants work not as passive recorders but as active artists who paint their versions of reality. New meanings and new ways of finding meaning emerge from slight alterations in old meanings and in old ways of finding meaning. To

watch infants engage in this process is to watch growth itself. If caregivers watch carefully, they will witness a mental life that is constantly changing, becoming more complex, yet at the same time maintaining continuity with the past. This chapter contains information about how infants think and what they think about—information that should make it easier for you to care for infants in ways that foster their development.

Three Points to Remember

When working with children, caregivers need to remember three major points:

1. *Children grow and develop at different rates and with different temperaments.* This fundamental truth is supported by research studies and theory in child development. So in discussing particular traits, do not pay too much attention to the child's age. Certain behaviors appear earlier for some children and later for others. Remember, too, that infants not only develop at different rates but also have different likes and dislikes. One infant, for example, enjoys sucking more than another infant does. Another infant shows signs of pleasure from being cuddled and does not suck as much as the first one. Still another

infant likes to be out of clothes and blankets more than most. They are unique individuals when they come into the world, and they remain that way as they grow.

2. *A child's intellect, emotions, and body do not develop separately.* The child grows and learns holistically, not in compartments. Motor, language, moral, intellectual, social, and emotional skills, attitudes, and stances blend to form the personal style of each child. Each area of development enables and influences development in other areas. Motor ability influences what children can explore, emotions flavor the language that they use, and mental pictures influence emotion. For example, between 18 and 24 months of age, most children have fairly good control of their body. They can walk and run, use their small muscles for detailed work, and are starting to control their bowels and bladder.

At the same time, children are developing skills in language. They know many more words than they can correctly say; and they are beginning to express desires, wishes, and resistance to the wishes of others.

Intellectually, these children are beginning to figure things out, and they have some basic mental symbols and ideas. They are starting to pretend and to understand concepts of past and present.

At the same time, they begin to see that choice of action is possible, and they often have a hard time when restrictions are placed on what they choose to do.

As they begin to stand on their own feet, walk in their own way, think their own thoughts, and express themselves in their own words, they become capable of many acts, and they change. Their simultaneous experiences in all the developmental domains help to build the dependent, independent, and interdependent self they are becoming.

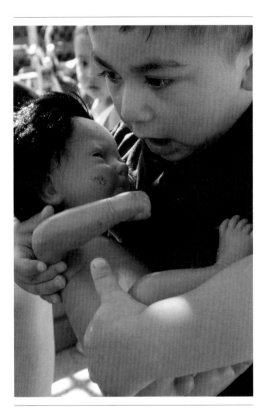

3. *Although adults obtain clues from infant behavior, all adult thought about how infants think describes infants in adult terms.* Adults have labeled various aspects of infant development, but those designations are just labels. Words like *autonomy, shame, initiative, independence,* and *guilt* are adult constructs that can illuminate certain aspects of infant behavior and development. Yet these

constructs can be deceptive if they lead to the belief that the experience of infants is the same as what comes to the minds of adults when they hear and think about such words as *autonomy* or *shame*.

Very young infants experience the world without knowledge of words and without the clarifying abstractions of adults. For example, infants do not experience trust as adults do. Trust is an adult concept that can be evaluated as good or bad, strong or weak, present or absent. The infant may be building a sense of trust that is not thought about or evaluated. Evaluation is the key to understanding the difference between infant and adult thinking. Young infants do not consciously reflect on experience, rate behavior, or judge themselves. They just live. Young infants do not realize anything about the process of development. They just develop. The older infant and toddler begin to evaluate but not with the specificity of the adult. Toddlers are more spontaneous and far less introspective than adults.

Infants and adults have different abilities; infants cannot experience the world in the same way that adults do. Similarly, adults can no longer experience the world as infants do. Sometimes, the adult view does a disservice to the infant. That is, most adults feel that their views and skills are better than those of infants and that the adults' view of life is more real than the infants'. This way of looking at infants invalidates the infants' experience as "less than" the adults' experience—one that should be worked on by adults and changed rather than given time

to develop. This view leads adults to try to shape infants, rush them through infancy to "more important" stages of life, push them to reach an adult's understanding of the world, and teach them. This view may interrupt important infant work and impose inappropriate demands, requests, and expectations. It may lead to insensitive and inappropriate caregiving.

Understanding the Thoughts of Infants and Toddlers

This exercise will help you understand infants. As you do it, try to feel the difference in quality and style of behavior between an infant and an adult. Close your eyes and point to where you think your mind is. This request may seem silly, but please do it. Most likely, you will point to a place on or near your head. Adults do this because of the cerebral nature of their understanding. If young infants were asked to point to their minds and were capable of understanding the exercise, they would most likely point to their tongues, eyes, or fingertips. Infants learn through their senses. Their learning processes are much less abstract than those of adults. The sensory system of learning used by infants requires more time, movement in space, and energy than the abstract system used by adults. This difference between infant behavior and adult behavior is a key to understanding the infant's view of the world. For the infant, understanding is mostly sensation; for the adult, mostly idea. The attention of young infants is mostly in the present, and their senses influence attention powerfully. As infants become older, their thinking processes gradually change.

Look at how the process works. Place a mobile above the crib of a four-month-old to eight-month-old infant so that the infant can touch it with his or her feet. Watch as the child waves his or her arms and kicks his or her legs to move the mobile. Periodically, take the mobile away for a minute or two and then return it to the crib. Watch what the infant does to show recognition. When the child has become familiar with the mobile, he or she will act differently toward it when it is returned. You will notice that when the infant sees it, he or she will move his or her arms or legs toward the mobile, in a partial motion of what was done in the past to make the mobile move. This partial motion is a motor recognition symbol, a memory of the mobile and past actions taken on it. As the child gets older, the motor symbol becomes more brief, and only a slight foot movement in recognition may appear. Finally, the motor sign is difficult to see at all. The internalizing that the child's motor memory goes through offers a glimpse of the work of sense and motor connections in an infant's mental activity. This gradual movement from sense to symbolic recognition is an example of how infants develop in the way they act on, understand, and recognize things.

The Intellectual Activity of Infancy

During the first 24 months of life, infants are actively constructing their world. An appreciation of what they are doing will help you to act appropriately. This section of the chapter summarizes cognitive development and learning during infancy.

Use of Reflexes

At birth infants use the skills they have brought from the womb: sucking, grasping, crying, hearing, seeing, smelling,

and specific reflexes, such as the rooting reflex (turning toward an object that touches the infant around the mouth and grasping that object with the mouth) and the "Moro" reflex (the dropped infant raises its arms and grasps). Very young infants have other skills as well. Infants avoid brightness. They can see up close but not far away; when they search with their eyes, their eyes move back and forth instead of up and down. They look at the edges of an object, not at the middle. They respond more to high tones when they are awake and to low tones when they are sleepy. They quickly come to recognize their mother's voice, identify smells, and prefer a mother's smell and voice to the voice and smell of a stranger. Young infants show preference for sweet liquids and for the human face. These skills are used for survival and for taking in information.

Altering Reflexes

As infants develop, their use of reflexes changes. Gradually, sucking becomes experiencing something satisfying to the taste and anticipating the nipple. Seeing

they show a marked increase in leg kicking, arm waving, banging, rubbing, and shaking to cause things to happen. At the same time, they start to put things into familiar categories. One of these categories might be things to kick and see movement; another, things to kick and hear that make sounds. At about this time, clear indications of intentional behavior appear.

Unquestioned Intention

Between seven and 12 months of age, infants show signs of unquestioned purpose. They move obstacles to get to a desired object and use tools to extend the impact of their body. At this time, they also show signs of anticipation; for example, they learn from seeing their mother put all the diapering materials away that she is about to leave the room. Infants may cry even before she goes because they anticipate her leaving.

Fear of Strangers

There are ways that infants recognize parents (for example, by smell) as early as the first day of life. Between seven and 12 months of age, infants become very good at recognizing those who have been caring for them and show signs of

becomes actively scanning the contrasts in light and dark. Hearing becomes listening—infants quiet their crying and body to be able to hear. The grasp changes to suit what is grasped. Unpleasant smells are avoided. Thumb sucking starts or increases as a chosen activity. Crying becomes a differentiated message that the parent can understand. By four months of age, the grasp has changed from a reflex closing of the hand when the palm is stimulated to a grasp that changes with the different objects or parts of the body grasped. The situation changes again when infants learn to keep their hands in view and try to look at things grasped and to grasp things seen. Early reflex behaviors have changed, infants have learned new skills through experience, and the skills learned have made the infants different.

Making Interesting Experiences Continue

At around four months of age, infants discover that experiences they caused by accident can also be caused on purpose. During this period,

not wanting to be with strangers. They become able to recognize a familiar adult and clearly prefer that person. This period can be particularly trying for the employed mother and for families who use unfamiliar adults as babysitters. For the infants, however, this period represents an intellectual and emotional breakthrough that helps them to recognize friends, relax in their presence, and build more permanent relationships.

Active Experimentation

Around their first birthday, infants start to treat objects differently. During the infant's brief past, objects were to be explored and understood. The properties and functions of an object were of prime importance. Now, infants fool around with objects and look for less obvious uses. At this time, they experiment with their own skills and seem to try to find new ways of doing things. One-year-old infants experiment and discover new ways of using tools and of getting what they want.

Insightful Learning

At approximately 18 months of age, infants spend time inventing. They imagine ways of acting that will serve their purpose. Crudely, they figure out a way of taking new action. Piaget observed that his child continually opened her mouth at 16 months of age while trying to get an attractive watch chain out of a matchbox (Ginsberg and Opper 1969). The action seemed to help her "think" about how to open the matchbox. Such action is typical when children begin to manipulate symbols in the mind.

Discoveries of Infancy

Part of the excitement of caring for infants and toddlers is watching them

become increasingly competent. So many lessons are being learned during infancy, and in such subtle ways, that adults often miss the lessons. It may be helpful for caregivers to cluster what is being learned into categories so that the child's learning activities can be more easily understood. What follows is a clustering based on the work of J. McVicker Hunt and Ina Uzguris (1975). They grouped learning activities that took place during the first 18 to 24 months of life (as described by Jean Piaget) into categories and placed them in order according to level of complexity.

Discovery One: Learning Schemes

During the first two years of life, infants begin to put things in groups and develop schemes of thought and action for exploring the world. They begin to develop familiarity with hard things, soft things, sticky things, light things, things that bounce, things that make noise, and so on. As they get older, they also learn to act differently with different kinds of things. Older infants treat different objects in different ways. They will not try to make aluminum foil stick to a block without using adhesive tape. They will also combine objects, put blocks in a container, or use a spoon to take sand from a sandbox. Learning the different properties of items continues into the preschool years. Infants touch, mouth, bang, pat, and throw things to discover the functions and properties of objects. Infants test the environment to see how it operates and learn new ways of acting in the process.

Discovery Two: Learning That Events Are Caused

Young infants do not make the connection between cause and effect. Often, they will bat something and look in puzzlement and disbelief as it rolls away. They do not make a connection between the action of batting and the movement of the object. Cause-and-effect understanding starts through simple body movements. First they come to understand the connection between cause and effect, and when they are about 15 months old they actively search for the mechanism that needs to be triggered to get a specific effect--what makes a light go on or what makes a sound happen. For example, they increasingly experiment with cause-and-effect by playing with light switches, radio dials, doorbells, "pop-up" toys, and so forth.

Discovery Three: Use of Tools

During infancy, children learn to extend themselves through the use of tools. At first, infants take in informa-tion through sight, smell, touch, and so forth. They use sense tools. Then infants start to act on things with the body. They grasp a bottle, bring it to their mouth, and suck. Infants also learn to use adults—for example, by putting something to be opened or rewound into the hand of a caregiver. Infants use adults as tools for getting food, toys, and comfort. Finally, infants use objects to help to get, hold onto, or explore things of interest—for example, standing on a box to reach the sink or pulling a leash to get a toy dog from under a table or chair.

Discovery Four: Object Permanence and Memory

From birth to about three to five months, the young infant does not search for objects removed from sight. Repeated contact with familiar objects—for example, a mother's face or a particular

rattle—helps the infant begin to realize that an object exists even when it is out of sight. When a child remembers that things still exist even when she cannot see or touch them, the child feels a greater sense of the permanence of her world. This knowledge deepens the child's relationships with loved ones. During the first year of life, the infant gradually is able to keep things in memory even when time has passed or he has been distracted by competing sensory experiences. This understanding deepens and becomes more complex throughout childhood.

Discovery Five: Learning How Objects Fill Space

Infants start to understand size and shape early, but they are not yet able to use this information to guide their behaviors. They also have trouble with the relationship between distance and perceived size and how much space an object will take up. Infants also have difficulty understanding that objects can change shape and that objects can be manipulated into different spaces. A good deal of infants' learning has to do with issues of space, density, distance, movement, and perspective. Infants build their understanding of spatial relationships in a number of ways, including bumping into walls, crawling into corners, getting stuck under tables, reaching for things beyond their grasp, and watching things closely.

Discovery Six: Imitation

During the first two years of life, infants become increasingly skillful at imitation—a powerful learning skill. Early in life infants imitate their own behaviors. Gradually, they mimic what they see—starting with general body activity—and they become increasingly selective and precise with their imitation.

Most infants' learning occurs through imitating parents and teachers. Infants learn to imitate sounds and actions. As infants move into the second year of life, they begin to imitate sequences of behavior. Eighteen-month-old infants combine sounds or imitate adults by using a cup, saucer, and spoon in pretending to drink coffee. Imitation is a powerful tool in learning socially appropriate behavior.

Facilitating Cognitive Development

The preceding six discoveries are themes of learning that infants and toddlers experience throughout the first two years of life. As children grow, they discover more about a theme and gain a more complete understanding of how that knowledge can be used to their advantage. Children make these discoveries naturally. They do not need to be taught about cause-and-effect or about space and distance.

Rather than teach infants and toddlers, become an interested and interesting play partner. At times, the infant will want to play an imitation game with you. The young infant may be most interested in your mirroring of sticking out his or her tongue at you, while the older infant may be fascinated by a finger game and song you initiate. At other times, the infant may learn about cause-and-effect by interacting with you. For example, if you respond, the young infant will begin to make the connection between his or her cry (the cause) and your coming close to comfort the infant (the effect). These are just some of the ways that your understanding and responsiveness are integral to the child's development. The chapters by Marc Bornstein and my other chapter in this guide (with Elita Amini Virmani) give further insight into the influence of the caregiver's action on the development of infants and toddlers.

In addition, part of facilitating children's development in general and intellectual development in particular involves offering choices of activities, respecting children's choices, and creating conditions for them to learn. Understanding the discoveries of infancy helps you (1) identify learning as it takes place so that you can avoid interfering with important intellectual activity; and (2) prepare materials and the environment so that the child will have a meaningful learning experience. The Introduction by Peter Mangione in this guide provides rich information on the foundations of cognitive development and learning in infants and toddlers.

When you look at infants as active learners who use their whole bodies (including their mouth, hands, feet, and skin) to discover the world around them, you see how important their actions are. Teaching becomes more interesting when you see the discoveries that children make each day and when you see yourself as a vital part of the children's fascinating enterprise of learning and discovery.

References

Ginsburg, H., and S. Opper. 1969. *Piaget's Theory of Intellectual Development: An Introduction*. Englewood Cliffs, NJ: Prentice-Hall.

Uzgiris, I. C., and J. McVicker Hunt. 1975. *Assessment in Infancy: Ordinal Scales of Psychological Development*. Champaign: University of Illinois Press.

Caregiver Responsiveness and Child Development and Learning: From Theory to Research to Practice

Marc H. Bornstein

*I*t was once commonly believed that responding to a baby's cries would make the baby fussier—or worse, a "household tyrant whose continual demands make a slave of the mother." Today, knowledge about infant care and its consequences has increased significantly. It is now understood that a baby's crying or smiling or reaching out sends a message about needs or likes or feelings, and it is natural for caregivers to respond to infants' signals.

Indeed, whether or not a caregiver responds to a baby may be a matter of the child's survival. At birth and for a long time afterward, human infants depend totally on adult caregivers to tend them. Not surprisingly, infants come equipped with a number of ways to communicate with their caregivers. Cries and smiles are two of the most powerful tools at babies' command. Cries tell a caregiver, "I'm hungry," "I'm tired," "I'm hurting," or "I need to be held." They bring the caregiver close to the child so that those needs can be met. Smiles say, "I like to be near you," "I like when you play with me," or "I like to hear you talk." They keep the caregiver close and promote and sustain interactions.

During the first year, babies also develop other signals or means of communicating that draw responses from their caregivers. For example, they begin to coo and babble, they learn to direct their

eyes to things and people of interest, and they start to point and reach. Eventually, they talk. The signals most commonly used by infants to communicate with their caregivers include the following:

- Distress vocalizing—crying, fretting, and fussing

- Nondistress vocalizing—cooing, babbling, and talking

- Visual attending—looking at objects and people in the environment

- Facial expressions—smiling and frowning

- Body movements—pointing at and reaching for objects and people

Indeed, even very young babies *expect* adults to respond to them. Using a "still-face" paradigm, researchers (Tronick

and others [1978] and Field and others [2007]) have shown over the years that infants are very sensitive to the absence of responsiveness in social interactions. An adult who interacts naturally with an infant and suddenly becomes non-responsive typically elicits demonstrative "upsetness" from the infant—more than does the adult's physically absenting their interaction altogether.

In short, infants activate many responses in adults through their voice, face, gaze, and gesture. In return, adult responsiveness fosters children's motivation to interact and, as will be seen, has positive effects on the course of children's development.

How should caregivers respond to children's signals? What are the consequences, if any, of caregivers' responsiveness? These are the main questions that are addressed in this article. First, *responsiveness* will be defined and typical characteristics identified. Next, the effects of responsiveness on infant crying will be examined as well as the short-term and long-term consequences for child cognitive development. Then, how responsiveness works and the origins of responsiveness in caregivers will be addressed.

Finally, ways to become a more responsive caregiver will be reviewed.

What Is Responsiveness?

Experts define *responsiveness* as a caregiver's verbal or nonverbal reactions to a child's signals. Responsiveness in normal, everyday exchanges has the following three main elements:

1. Contingency— The adult's action depends on or occurs in reaction to the child's action (responsive adult activities do not occur at just any time).

2. Appropriateness—The adult's action is conceptually related to the child's action and is geared to fulfill a child need (not every adult action does).

3. Promptness—The adult's action follows the child's action closely in time (so that the child learns to associate the two).

Responsiveness does not include a caregiver's act that just happens to follow a child's act, nor does it include a caregiver's spontaneous stimulation. In neither of those two cases does the caregiver's act depend on or occur in relation to the child's act. So, being responsive means not simply interacting with baby, but being contingent, appropriate, and prompt, too. For example, when a four-month-old turns to his or her caregiver and starts to coo, a responsive caregiver would make eye contact with the child and coo back— "have a conversation." If, after a time, that same child starts to fuss or averts his or her gaze, the responsive caregiver knows that the conversation has ended. Responsive caregivers listen to children's signals and then adjust their behavior contingently, appropriately, and promptly in response to those signals.

Researchers who study responsiveness break down adult–infant interaction into three separate but related events:

- Child action
- Caregiver response
- Effect on the child

This analysis provides a framework for taking a closer look at responsiveness and its effects. Keeping this structure in mind while caring for infants and young children can be helpful in reading their signals and understanding the consequences of caregiver responses.

What Are Some Typical Characteristics of Responsiveness?

Some people are very responsive to children, some are moderately so, and some seldom respond. For example, in one study with infants only five months of age, Marc Bornstein and Catherine Tamis-LeMonda (1989) found that some

caregivers were responsive during less than 5 percent of the time they were observed, whereas others were responsive during as much as 75 percent of the time. Surprisingly, this variation is true of individuals in the same social class and with approximately the same years of schooling. Responsiveness may be shaped by education, but once a person knows how to be optimally responsive, the educational level really does not matter as much as the behavior.

A caregiver's response typically varies with the age of the child and the type of child activity the caregiver is responding to. A caregiver's initial response to a young baby's distress usually takes the form of "social soothing": that is, holding and patting the baby. Thus, a crying infant is most likely to experience contact with the caregiver and soothing social interaction. By contrast, when caregivers respond to an infant's coos and babbles, they themselves typically vocalize, often

imitating the child's sounds. When they respond to an infant's attempts at exploration, caregivers generally help the baby to become better oriented to objects the baby wants to explore, or they bring objects to the baby. Finally, when caregivers respond to a baby's bids for social interaction, they tend to stimulate and engage the infant in affectionate social play. Caregivers use a more complex set of signals and responses for older toddlers than they do for young infants.

Notably, a study (Bornstein et al. 1992) showed that the characteristics of maternal responsiveness to infant activity during home-based naturalistic interactions of mother–infant dyads in New York City, Paris, and Tokyo are pretty similar in some important ways. All mothers respond to infants' exploration of the environment with encouragement to the environment, to infants' vocalizing nondistress with vocalizations and imitation, and to infants' vocalizing distress with nurturance.

How Does Responsiveness Affect a Baby's Expressions of Distress?

Because crying is one of the most prominent signals that a baby is capable of producing initially, the frequency and manner in which caregivers respond to cries historically have been of uppermost concern. Before responsiveness from caregivers became a subject of research, it was commonly believed that caregivers who responded too often or quickly to a child's cries would "reinforce" or reward crying, and the child would learn to cry more often. Silvia Bell and Mary Salter Ainsworth (1972) decided to see whether this commonly held belief was true. They periodically observed a group of mothers naturally interacting with their newborn babies across the first year of life. By the time the children celebrated their first birthday, Bell and Ainsworth found that toddlers whose mothers had responded more often to their cries as babies actually cried less often, not more.

One possible explanation for this unexpected result is that, when caregivers responded to children's signals, children learned that they were not helpless but rather that their behaviors had an effect on the world. They learned that they could control their environment in a predictable and reliable way. Bell and Ainsworth (1972) hypothesized that, as infants matured, they learned to substitute more sophisticated means of communication for crying; hence, they cried less than children whose caregivers did not impart this sense of control by being as responsive. Indeed, by the end of a child's first year, children of responsive parents not only cried less, but their noncry communications were more varied, subtle, and clear. These children communicated more distinctly and understandably using facial expressions, gestures, and nondistress vocalization.

Bell and Ainsworth (1972) concluded that maternal responsiveness to infants' signals promotes a feeling of competence and confidence in children that fosters the development of communication and encourages the development of children's cognitive skills. Since this work, evidence has accumulated to support the hypothesis that babies of responsive caregivers may be at an advantage in a host of ways—for example, in learning, exploration, and motivation. Responsiveness from caregivers appears to benefit the social and emotional development of children too. These issues are examined in the next sections.

How Does Being Responsive Affect the Child's Cognitive and Social–Emotional Development?

Being responsive to a child affects the child's cognitive and social–emotional development, just as, reciprocally, children who do not experience responsive caregiving suffer in these domains of development. Key to children's development of wholesome relationships is their early "secure attachment" to a primary caregiver, and key to attachment is the caregiver's sensitivity and responsiveness. Infants and young children can display different types of attachment patterns— secure, avoidant, ambivalent, disorganized. And their attachment status depends, to some degree, on the quality of care— sensitive responsiveness—they have received. Indeed, it was on the basis of studies of maternal deprivation (in institutionalized care, because of war) that John Bowlby (1969, 1973, 1980) formulated attachment theory. Children who are securely at-

tached adjust more soundly, are more socially competent with peers and other adults, and perhaps develop more positive romantic relationships later.

Michael Lewis and Susan Goldberg (1969) were among the first researchers to notice a positive relation between responsive caregiving and better cognitive performance in children. They found that three-month-old babies whose mothers responded more frequently to their vocalizations tended to learn about new things in their environment by looking at them more quickly than did children of less responsive mothers. Subsequent research studies confirmed that maternal responsiveness is positively associated with children's cognitive development. For example, Michael Goldstein and his colleagues (2009) found that the development of children whose mothers were discriminating in their responding to infants' earliest sounds and babbling was changed by mothers' responding. Bornstein and

his colleagues (1989, 1992, 2008) have studied responsiveness extensively in the United States and abroad and found that responsiveness has broader short-term and long-term cognitive benefits for babies. Children of mothers who were more responsive to their nondistress signals (such as vocalization, facial expression, and movements) during the middle of the child's first year and at one and two years of age tended to show advanced language. Four-year-old children whose mothers had been more responsive when the children were infants solved problems more efficiently and scored higher on a standardized intelligence test than did their peers with less responsive mothers.

Caregivers' responsiveness to children's vocalizations seems to be particularly significant to the development of language. For example, one early study reported that caregivers who responded to infants' vocalizations had children who tended to vocalize more fluently to a toy than did children with less responsive caregivers. Kathleen Bloom, Allan Russell, and Karen Wassenberg (1987) found that caregiver responsiveness helps to instill conversational rhythm in babies. When an adult experimenter responded to three-month-old infants' vocalizations and maintained a turn-taking or "speak–listen" pattern, babies tended to pause between their own vocalizations. These babies also tended to produce more mature speechlike sounds than did a group of babies whose sounds were mostly ignored. Also, Michael Goldstein, Jennifer Schwade, and Marc Bornstein (2009) found that infants' own vocalizing depended on feedback from caregivers. All these were experimental studies with results from the laboratory. However, they demonstrate that infants and young children are sensitive to the reactions of others, concluding, as research such as that of Luigi Girolametto and Elaine Weitzman (2002) showed, that infants are sensitive to their child care providers and not just to their parents.

How powerful is caregiver responsiveness? Tamis-LeMonda and Bornstein (2002) looked at five language milestones, including when children understood their first word, spoke their first word, reached a vocabulary of 50 words, put two words together, and talked about the past. Children whose mothers were more responsive reached these developmental milestones as much as six months earlier than children of less responsive mothers. At the same time, caregiver responsiveness is selective. The two investigators also compared mothers' responsiveness to their children's play versus mothers' responsiveness to their children's language. Responsiveness to children's play improved children's play but not their language, whereas responsiveness to children's language improved children's language but not their play. Maternal responsiveness is robust and specific in its effects on child development.

Leila Beckwith and Saralee Cohen (1989) studied responsiveness in the caregivers of preterm infants and found similar positive effects. Infants who were more skillful at nine months in sensorimotor tasks (such as searching for a hidden object, using one object as a means to obtain another, or inventing a solution to a problem) at one month of age had experienced more mutual caregiver–infant gazing (that is, looking intently at one another); at three months, more interchanges of smiling during mutual gazing and more responsiveness; and at eight months, greater levels of social interaction, including more responsiveness. As additional

evidence of the long-term effects of being responsive to infant vocalizations, Beckwith and Cohen followed their families over time. Those mothers who were more verbally responsive to preterm children's nondistress vocalizations, when the children were eight months and 24 months of age, had children who tended to have higher IQ scores at 12 years of age.

In addition, responsiveness appears to exert similar effects across different cultures. Bornstein and his colleagues Kazuo Miyake, Hiroshi Azuma, Catherine S. LeMonda, and Sueko Toda conducted a study (1990) with mothers and children in Sapporo, Japan. Japanese children whose mothers were more responsive to them when they were four to five months old scored higher on a standardized mental achievement test at two and one-half years of age than did children with less responsive mothers. Leila Paavola and

her colleagues (2005) in Finland also found that maternal responsiveness during the prelinguistic stage of children's communicative competence predicts their early communicative and linguistic skills.

Of course, many people had suspected (mostly on account of studies of infants reared in institutions) that children deprived of social responsiveness normally fare poorly in development; but factors apart from responsiveness were also thought to undermine the possible happy futures of these children. Such babies tend to be undernourished and understimulated too. However, a study conducted by Craig Ramey and his colleagues (1975) pointed to responsiveness as a significant factor. He gave one group of failure-to-thrive infants a nutritional supplement and a comparable group the same nutritional supplement plus weekly responsive stimulation. The second group subsequently performed better than the first group on a learning task. On this basis, Ramey and his colleagues (1975) suggested that the quality of both nutrition and social responsiveness can reduce the effects of development al retardation.

Ramey also noticed something else intriguing about the children in the study: they showed a marked change in their social and emotional demeanor. Instead of being apathetic, children appeared alert and responsive. Ramey (1975) could only speculate on the cause, but they suspected that responsive stimulation played a part. In the time since, numerous studies have shown that being responsive to a child has positive effects on the child's social and emotional life, an action that in turn can create a better environment for children's development.

Some domains of social–emotional development in children are closely related to their cognitive development. For example, having a conscience and possessing social skills (such as reading others' emotions) depend on cognitive development. Both in turn depend on experience the child has with a responsive caregiver. Laura Steelman, Mike Assel, Paul Swank, Karen Smith, and Susan Landry (2002) found that early maternal responsiveness predicted children's development of social skills. More specifically, Grazyna Kochanska, David Forman, Nazan Aksan, and Stephen Dunbar (2005) learned through their research that early mother–child mutual responsiveness was a pathway to children's moral emotions, conduct, and conscience. Parenting that is responsive is credited with fostering many valued developmental outcomes, including emotional security, social facility, symbolic competence, verbal ability, and intellectual achievement.

cessfully solving problems. Infants who have prior experience with stimulation within their control learn more competently and efficiently in new situations than do infants without such experience.

How Does Responsiveness Work?

Research studies have shown that responsiveness exerts beneficial effects in development, but *how* it does so is not always clear. On this aspect researchers are more tentative and speculative. But, as seen from the discussion thus far, responsiveness might have an effect through several possible mechanisms.

1. Caregiver responsiveness might empower children by instilling in them feelings of control and effectance; that is, children might learn that they have a positive effect on their environment. This discovery, in turn, might increase children's motivation to learn and their confidence in suc-

2. Responsive caregiving might promote self-regulation in children, which facilitates their attention and learning.

3. Responsive caregiving might provide caregivers and children with closely shared opportunities to learn about one another and thereby assist children's learning.

4. Responsiveness may elevate a child's mood, making the child more open to learning.

5. Last but by no means least, responsiveness may promote caregiver–infant attachment, which in turn determines the degree to which the infant feels secure to explore and learn about his or her world.

The point here is that it is not simply that responsive mothers have children who are more advanced; mothers and their babies do share genes. Karen Hardy-Brown and Robert Plomin (1985) found that mothers' verbal responses to the vocalizations of their adopted one-year-olds predict children's communicative development. This finding pinpoints the effectiveness of responsiveness and separates it from alternative interpretations based on shared genetics between parent and child. The research also means that the mechanism of action of responsiveness does not depend on the caregiver being biologically related to the child. The *responsiveness of children's caregivers* is what matters the most to children's development.

Where Does Caregiver Responsiveness Come From?

Because of the important role that responsiveness seems to play in child development, it is reasonable to ask why some caregivers are more responsive than other caregivers. Some believe that caregiver responsiveness represents purely biological functioning; others, that caregiver responsiveness develops from experience. Some believe that women are naturally more responsive than men; others, that all members of the human community—men, women, and children alike—are responsive but in different degrees.

The Nobel Prize–winning ethologist Konrad Lorenz hypothesized that responsiveness is an unlearned instinct in adults, one that is deeply embedded in the psyche and automatically excited by key physical features of an infant, such as the infant's large head in relation to the size of the rest of the body, bulbous forehead, soft elastic skin, and cry. Lorenz (1943, 1971) thought that those traits spontaneously and involuntarily "release" inborn emotional and motor reactions in adults. Indeed, that is why Lorenz asserted that human beings feel so strongly not only about human babies but about kittens, pups, and animal babies in general, because the very young of many species share the same "babyish" attributes.

There is also growing evidence that hormones play a role in the expression of human responsiveness (Feldman 2012). For example, the neurohormone oxytocin predicts mothers' sensitive behavior with newborn babies and how they coordinate with the newborn state. Fathers' higher levels of prolactin are associated with more alert and positive responses to infant cries, and their lower levels of testosterone explain their affective responses to infant cries (Fleming and others 2002).

Biology aside, it is clear that caregivers in the same culture and from different cultures vary in the degree to which they are responsive. At one end of the spectrum, maternal responsiveness is essentially nonexistent in some cultural groups (villages in Guatemala and New Guinea, for example). Although responsiveness exists in most cultures, caregivers in some

cultures are regularly more responsive than caregivers in other cultures. So, at the other end of the responsiveness spectrum, Kung San (in Botswana) caregivers respond almost immediately to almost every infant signal. By contrast, Gusii (in Kenya) caregivers reportedly respond to fewer than 10 percent of infants' vocalizations. Overall, American mothers respond to between 50 percent and 80 percent of a variety of infants' and young children's actions; in Western societies (Australia, Western Europe, and North America), responsiveness still varies considerably.

Many factors play a role in whether and how caregivers behave responsively (Bornstein 1989). They include characteristics of the caregiver (for example, an empathic and adaptable individual may be more responsive); the circumstances under which the caregiver is functioning (for example, a caregiver with just a few children in his or her charge may be able to be more responsive than a caregiver with many children); and characteristics of the child (for example, a child who is irritable and difficult to soothe alters caregiver responsiveness). Postpartum depression is common—it appears after 12 percent of births—and depressed mothers are less responsive to their infants. Nanmathi Manian and Marc Bornstein (2009) studied the effects of mothers' nonresponsiveness on their infants' development. By five months, infants of depressed mothers already show different patterns of social interaction and ability to regulate their own behavior. Many factors determine the responsiveness of a caregiver to a child.

One variable that has been found to have an effect on the expression of responsiveness is experience with children. The amount of experience a caregiver has with children helps to determine the degree of responsiveness to an infant's noncry vocalizations. For example, Ole Wasz-Höckert and his colleagues (1964) some time ago showed experimentally that experienced women (regardless of parental status) identified types of cries better and that men with child-rearing experience performed better than men without experience in identifying specific types of cries. Holder (1988) also studied the role of experience in responding to infant cries and found experienced nonparents equally good as parents at decoding the meaning of cries.

Accumulating experience with a particular child makes a difference. A group of mothers watched an assessment administered to their infants, received an explanation of the assessment scale, and learned about their infants' performance on the assessment. Later, mothers in this group showed significantly enhanced responsiveness while interacting with their infants as compared with a control group who had simply learned about children's toys and furnishings. In turn, the increased responsiveness of mothers was reflected in infants' own responsiveness. Babies whose mothers had learned about their behavior showed gains in alertness, positive affect and mood, and visual responsiveness to their mothers. It seems that getting to know children can help caregivers become more attuned to children's needs, knowledge that apparently leads to more alert and responsive children.

How Can a Caregiver Become More Responsive?

To become responsive, a caregiver must be able to perceive an infant's signals, understand their meaning, and then respond contingently, appropriately, and promptly. The first step, *perceiving*, is straightforward. Caregivers have to be available and attentive. They should also know something about what they are looking at and listening for. To some degree, this knowledge comes with experience. Also, reading books on child development and ways to care for children is certainly helpful.

Interpreting what is perceived is a little harder: *Is the baby crying because he is hungry, overstimulated, or needs to be held?* Finding the answer to this question comes not just from learning about babies generally, but from learning about the particular baby being cared for and the caregiving context. Each child comes to every setting with her own temperament, daily rhythm, likes, and dislikes. By carefully watching the child, over time and in different contexts, a caregiver will come to understand that child's personality and will then be able to decipher that child's messages better and respond more effectively. Jan Karrass and Julia Braungart-Rieker (2003) found that children's temperament plays a role, along with responsive parenting, as agents in children's early language development.

The final step—being able to respond contingently, appropriately, and prompt-ly—is just an extension of understanding what the child needs. Once a caregiver understands the message, the response should follow suit. If a child looks at a caregiver with a big, broad smile, he probably would like the caregiver to smile back and maybe engage in social play. If the child then changes mood and starts to avert the caregiver's gaze, he is probably saying, "I'm tired; I think I've had enough for now" and would like some quiet time. A toddler who moves from object to object, pointing with her index finger and glancing over to the caregiver, probably wants him to name each item. And when the toddler looks at a caregiver and says "Ba," the child probably would like the caregiver to look at her and say "Ba" back. A toddler who points to a ball and says "Ba" might like it if the caregiver said "ball" or better yet expand and say "Yes, it's a ball. See how high it bounces."

As caregivers get to know each child, they learn to fine-tune their responses. For some children, social interaction might call for tickling or other rough-and-tumble play; other children might prefer quiet verbal games in response. If a caregiver is attentive and receptive to children's signals, those signals will tell her what the children need and want, when they would like stimulation and when they do not, when they need to be held, when they want more freedom to explore, when they are happy, and when they are sad. The more caregivers can communicate to children that they have heard the message and understand, the more responsive caregivers will be.

Is it always the case that an important caregiving practice such as responsiveness is "better" insofar as it occurs more often? Perhaps less is more, or some is more. Bornstein and his colleague Nanmathi Manian (2012) studied mothers' responsiveness to infants in relation to global judgments of their parenting sensitivity. They discovered that mothers who were not responsive enough and mothers who were always responsive were rated less sensitive to infants. Mothers who were responsive at moderate levels were judged most sensitive. Clinically depressed mothers are unresponsive to infant signals and fail to provide infants with contingent, appropriate, and prompt stimulation. Children of depressed mothers are at risk for poor development, in part because of their mothers' unresponsive parenting. By contrast, overresponsiveness may be both overstimulating to children and developmentally inappropriate. Consequently, overcontingent parenting fails to instill a child with the confidence and ability to self-regulate and explore and prevents or inhibits the child from developing coping skills. Mothers who are overresponsive and underresponsive are rated as less sensitive, whereas mid-levels of maternal responsiveness are rated as optimally sensitive.

What Has Been Learned from Research About Responsiveness?

Findings from research converge in showing the powerful role that responsiveness plays over the development of a broad range of children's competencies. Responsiveness is a central parenting construct that is a common characteristic of caregiving around the world. Caregivers need to display the contingent, appropriate, and prompt reactions typically associated with responsiveness. Persistent child-rearing practices are often credited with changing the course of child development. To be responsive, caregivers need to know the children in their care by developing a close relationship and being attentive and receptive to a child's signals.

Responsiveness is a deceptively uncomplicated concept. Hidden, however, are the telling and powerful consequences responsiveness portends—not only for the infant's survival but also for the child's positive development of social self-confidence and intellectual capability.

References

Beckwith, L., and S. E. Cohen. 1989. "Maternal Responsiveness with Preterm Infants and Later Competency." In *Maternal Responsiveness: Characteristics and Consequences*. Edited by M. H. Bornstein. San Francisco: Jossey-Bass, 75–87.

Bell, S. M., and M. D. Ainsworth. 1972. "Infant Crying and Maternal Responsiveness." *Child Development* 43 (4): 1171–90.

Bloom, K., A. Russell, and K. Wassenberg. 1987. "Turn Taking Affects the Quality of Infant Vocalizations." *Journal of Child Language* (14): 211–27.

Bornstein, M. H., ed. 1989. *Maternal Responsiveness: Characteristics and Consequences*. San Francisco: Jossey-Bass.

Bornstein, M. H., and N. Manian. 2012. "Material Responsiveness and Sensitivity Reconsidered: Some Is More." Unpublished manuscript. Eunice Kennedy Shriver National Institute of Child Health and Human Development.

Bornstein, M. H., C. Hendricks, O. M. Haynes, and K. M. Painter. 2007. "Maternal Sensitivity and Child Responsiveness: Associations with Social Context, Maternal Characteristics, and Child Characteristics in a Multivariate Analysis." *Infancy* 12:189–223.

Bornstein, M. H., K. Miyake, H. Azuma, C. S. Tamis-LeMonda, and S. Toda. 1990. *Responsiveness in Japanese Mothers: Consequences and Characteristics*. Annual Report of the Research and Clinical Center for Child Development, 15–26. Sapporo, Japan: Hokkaido University.

Bornstein, M. H., and C. S. Tamis-LeMonda. 1989. "Maternal Responsiveness and Cognitive Development in Children." In *Maternal Responsiveness: Characteristics and Consequences*, edited by M. H. Bornstein, 49–61. San Francisco: Jossey-Bass.

———. 1997. "Maternal Responsiveness and Infant Mental Abilities: Specific Predictive Relations." *Infant Behavior and Development* 20:283–96.

Bornstein, M. H., C. S. Tamis-LeMonda, C. S. Hahn, and O. M. Haynes. 2008. "Maternal Responsiveness to Very Young Children at Three Ages: Longitudinal Analysis of a Multidimensional Modular and Specific Parenting Construct." *Developmental Psychology* 44:867–74.

Bornstein, M. H., C. S. Tamis-LeMonda, J. Tal, P. Ludemann, S. Toda, C. W. Rahn, M. G. Pecheux, H. Azuma, and D. Vardi. 1992. "Maternal Responsiveness to Infants in Three Societies: The United States, France, and Japan." *Child Development* 63:808–21.

Bowlby, J. 1969. *Attachment*. Vol. 1. New York: Basic Books.

———. 1973. *Separation: Anxiety and Anger*. Vol. 2. London: Hogarth Press.

———. 1980. *Loss: Sadness and Depression*. Vol. 3. London: Hogarth Press.

Feldman, R. 2012. "Bio-behavioral Synchrony: A Model for Integrating Biological and Microsocial Behavioral Processes in the Study of Parenting. *Parenting Science and Practice* 12.

Field, T., M. Hernandez-Reif, M. Diego, L. Feijo, Y. Vera, K. Gil, and C. Sanders. 2007. "Still-Face and Separation Effects on Depressed Mother-Infant Interactions." *Infant Mental Health Journal* 28 (3): 314–23.

Fleming, A. S., C. Corter, J. Stallings, and M. Steiner. 2002. "Testosterone and Prolactin Are Associated with Emotional Responses to Infant Cries in New Fathers." *Hormones and Behavior* 42:399–413.

Girolametto, L., and E. Weitzman. 2002. "Responsiveness of Child Care Providers in Interactions with Toddlers and Preschoolers." *Language, Speech, and Hearing Services in Schools* 33 (4): 268–81.

Goldstein, M. H., J. A. Schwade, and M. H. Bornstein. 2009. "The Value of Vocalizing: Five-Month-Old Infants Associate Their Own Noncry Vocalizations with Responses from Caregivers." *Child Development* 80:636–44.

Gros-Louis, J., M. J. West, M. H. Goldstein, and A. P. King. 2006. "Mothers Provide Differential Feedback to Infants' Prelinguistic Sounds." *Interna-*

tional Journal of Behavioral Development 30 (6): 509–16.

Hardy-Brown, K., and R. Plomin. 1985. Infant Communicative Development: Evidence from Adoptive and Biological Families for Genetic and Environmental Influences on Rate Differences." *Developmental Psychology* 21 (2): 378–85.

Holden, G. W. 1988. "Adults' Thinking About a Child-Rearing Problem: Effects of Experience, Parental Status, and Gender. *Child Development* 59:1623–32.

Karrass, J., and J. M. Braungart-Rieker. 2003. "Parenting and Temperament as Interacting Agents in Early Language Development." *Parenting: Science and Practice* 3 (3): 235–59.

Kochanska, G., D. R. Forman, N. Aksan, S. B. Dunbar. 2005. "Pathways to Conscience: Early Mother–Child Mutually Responsive Orientation and Children's Moral Emotion, Conduct, and Cognition." *Journal of Child Psychology and Psychiatry* 46 (1): 19–34.

Lewis, M., and S. Goldberg. 1969. "Perceptual–Cognitive Development in Infancy: A Generalized Expectancy Model as a Function of the Mother–Infant Interaction. *Merrill-Palmer Quarterly* 15:81–100.

Lorenz, K. 1943. Die angeborenen Formen möglicher Erfahrung (Innate Form of Potential 685 Experiences). *Z Tiepsychol.* 5:235–309, 686.

———. 1971. *Studies in Animal and Human Behavior.* Vol. 2. London: Methuen.

Manian, N., and M. H. Bornstein. 2009. "Dynamics of Emotion in Infants of Clinically Depressed and Nondepressed Mothers." *Journal of Child Psychology and Psychiatry* 50:1410–18.

Paavola, L., S. Kunnari, and I. Moilanen. 2005. "Maternal Responsiveness and Infant Intentional Communication: Implications for the Early Communicative and Linguistic Development." *Child: Care, Health and Development* 31 (6): 727–35.

Ramey, C. T., R. H. Starr, J. Pallas, C. F. Whitten, and V. Reed. 1975. "Nutrition, Response-Contingent Stimulation, and the Maternal Deprivation Syndrome: Results of an Early Intervention Program. *Merrill-Palmer Quarterly* 21 (1): 45–53.

Steelman, L. M., M. A. Assel, P. R. Swank, K. E. Smith, and S. H. Landry. 2002. "Early Maternal Warm Responsiveness as a Predictor of Child Social Skills: Direct and Indirect Paths of Influence over Time." *Journal of Applied Developmental Psychology* 23 (2): 135–56.

Tamis-LeMonda, C. S., and M. H. Bornstein. 2002. "Maternal Responsiveness and Early Language Acquisition." In *Advances in Child Development and Behavior,* edited by R. V. Kail and H. W. Reese, Vol. 29: 89–127. New York: Academic Press.

Tamis-LeMonda, C. S., M. H. Bornstein, and L. Baumwell. 2001. "Maternal Responsiveness and Children's Achievement of Language Milestones." *Child Development* 72:748–67.

Tamis-LeMonda, C. S., M. H. Bornstein, L. Baumwell, and A. M. Damast. 1996. "Responsive Parenting in the Second Year: Specific Influences on Children's Language and Play." *Early Development and Parenting* 5:173–83.

Tronick E., H. Als, L. Adamson, S. Wise, and T. B. Brazelton. 1978. "The Infant's Response to Entrapment between Contradictory Messages in Face-to-Face Interaction." *Journal of American Academy of Child and Adolescent Psychiatry* 17:1–13.

Learning During the Early Months

J. Ronald Lally and Elita Amini Virmani

Over the past 40 years, developmental psychologists and child development researchers have begun to discover many of the remarkable capacities of young infants. Far from John Locke's seventeenth-century conceptualization of babies as "tabula rasa," we now know with a great deal of certainty that babies are not blank slates to be written on by knowing adults or even empty vessels to be filled up with knowledge. Rather, babies come into the world with skills, competencies, and motivation to learn. Right from birth they are trying to figure out the way the world works. What we have recently found out is that a great deal of early learning happens through the give-and-take of everyday interactions with their primary caregivers. Research on the brain suggests that infants arrive in the world curious, wired to connect with others and to use those connections for learning.

Even before a baby is born, hundreds of billions of brain cells have formed and start connecting with each other. By the time babies are eight months old, they will have produced about 1,000 trillion connections—synapses—many more than they will end up with in adulthood. As the baby goes through life, depending on the types of experiences he or she will have, about half of these synapse connections will die off while others will grow strong and efficient. By starting with an overabundance of connections, babies' brains are ready to be shaped by the experiences they will encounter. The focus of this chapter is on just how, during the earliest months of life, positive connections are maintained and strengthened and how primary caregivers can best support early learning.

Recent Neuroscience

Of interest to neuroscientists, particularly those studying the brains of babies since the year 2000, is the influence that early experience has on the development of the early maturing right brain. During the last trimester of the prenatal period, and through the end of the second year of life, the right hemisphere—which is largely responsible for emotional and social functioning—undergoes a growth spurt (Schore 2001, 2003, 2005). Siegel

(2001) proposes that during this period early social and emotional exchanges between infants and caregivers directly impact the brain circuits related to the infant's capacity to cope with stress and deal with novelty. Greenspan (1990) contends that a baby's first motivation is to get his or her emotional needs met, and that this motivation drives skill development not only for emotional and social development but also for intellectual and language development. According to Greenspan, "It is the pleasure and delight that babies get from interaction with people that drive them to relate to people more frequently and more skillfully" (Greenspan 1990, 17). Recent neuroscience has validated Greenspan's clinical findings with hard science showing that a baby's emotional need to build, sustain, and use relationships drives communication and motivates language use (Schore 2005, 2001). What recent research tells us about early learning is that the interactions babies have with their principal caregivers positively or negatively impact the developing brain, both in terms of the brain's structure and overall function (Schore 2001). The brain gets shaped through babies' interactions with those who care for them. Specifically, the quality of the care babies receive from their primary caregivers influences the babies' ability to successfully or unsuccessfully attach to other human beings (Sroufe 1996), regulate their impulses, learn how to communicate with others, and search for an intellectual understanding of the world into which they are born.

The avenue for shaping the brain is the relationship. The information communicated through the emotional interactions in these early relationships is what shapes the brain (Siegel 2001). What is now understood is that early exchanges with primary caregivers, both parents and teachers, play a particularly important role in building the foundation for future learning. The information that gets processed in those exchanges, together with the emotional quality of the exchanges, influences the establishment of neuronal connections.

The Importance of Early Relationships for Early Learning

We are coming to view the brain as much more than the home of the intellect. We now understand that the brain is a "social brain," dependent on a rich social and emotional environment for growth and development (Brothers 1990). Cognitive capacity grows as part of this social brain through babies' participation in early social–emotional exchanges. For example, in a back-and-forth exchange,

a baby will develop (intellectual) strategies to prolong the feeling of pleasure (emotions) experienced and learn ways of acting (intellectual) to trigger particular types of emotional responses from his or her caregiver. Cognitive skills and language skills develop as the baby builds and uses relationships.

Additionally, secure relationships provide safety for exploration. For the young baby to truly take advantage of learning opportunities that arise, both physical and emotional safety are necessary. When young infants have internalized the sense that their parent or teacher will be available to help them calm down when too frustrated or too upset, babies are more able to explore new things and new people in the environment. When a baby's emotional expectations are violated (e.g., caregiver does not respond when expected to), it can trouble the baby so much that opportunities for cognitive growth are shut down. When babies receive the emotional help they expect when they need it, they will be more likely to be open to learning from the novel and even moderately stressful events that occur each day. Secure relationships with caring adults are the context in which infants become confident enough to intellectually explore the people and objects in their world.

Unique Aspects of Baby Learning

Learning in infancy is different from how older children or adults learn. Alison Gopnik, a leading researcher in the field of infant cognition, states, "Babies aren't trying to learn one particular skill or set of facts; instead, they are drawn to anything new, unexpected, or informative" (Gopnik 2009). To benefit from the experience of exploring new and unexpected things in their environment, infants must

have the social and emotional foundation to do so. Often this is the kind of invisible part of early learning that we take for granted. While seemingly simple, the research suggests that in addition to establishing a secure relationship with the infant, the best thing a caregiver can do is to talk to, play with, and pay close attention to infants and to their exploration of the world (Gopnik, Meltzoff, and Kuhl 1999). Infant learning is not taught in the same adult-directed way as one might imagine in teaching a child how to read or how to learn multiplication tables. Infant learning is about discovery and ensuring that the physical and social environment is set up for the process to happen in a way that the infant feels safe to take on new challenges.

Although cognitive development and social–emotional development often happen in concert with each other, how babies react to situations is not the same. Babies are wired to seek and form relationships, send signals of need, and pursue nurturance. They expect their messages to be heard, understood, and responded to adequately (National Research Council & Institute of Medicine 2000; Belsky, Spritz, and Crnic 1994; Honig 2002; Sroufe 1996). When their expectations are violated—when they do not receive the expected response—they fall apart. Ed Tronick's (2005) still-face experiment with babies is a classic example of this finding. Mothers whom he instructed to, only for a brief period of time, not respond to a child's signals can cause great emotional distress. Babies expect their signals to be read and understood; if that does not happen, it is deeply disturbing to them. In the area of social–emotional development, when children's expectations are not met, they are thrown off course and have little interest in doing anything else but establishing a relationship that works for them. Little time is spent in independent discovery of the environment and objects in it if their emotional needs are not met.

With cognitive development, the experience of having expectations violated is not negative; instead, it motivates the child to see why his or her expectations are violated. Violated expectations trigger curiosity and motivate the child to figure out why something is not acting the way he or she thinks it should. For instance, if a ball drops at a much faster speed than usual, an infant will look surprised or pause as if to say, "Huh? That didn't happen the way I expected it to."

As another example, consider an infant who is lying on his stomach and bats at a toy in front of him. The infant presumes, *If I make contact with the ball, then it will move*. If the ball moves, then the infant's hypothesis has been confirmed and little new learning takes place. However, if the ball does not move, this violates the infant's intellectual expectation, which allows for the process of discovery and hypothesis testing to begin. Discovery happens when babies expect one thing to happen, yet something else happens, and they are puzzled.

Experiences in which a baby recognizes that the same thing happens again and again become expected by the baby and soon become of little interest to her. It is the novel experiences, however, that infants enjoy and find interesting. Repeated, positive emotional experiences are pleasurable to the baby and are pursued with great interest. By understanding this difference in a baby's reaction to cognitive and social–emotional experiences, we go a long way toward understanding the role of an infant care teacher or parent during the early months.

The Role of Infant Care Teachers in Early Learning

What infant care teachers need to understand is that they must simultaneously meet the social–emotional expectations of their babies while creating interesting environments and experiences in which babies can test out their intellectual expectations. Understanding that the baby is both emotionally vulnerable and intellectually competent leads teachers to set up intellectual challenges that take place in the context of secure relationships. Infant care teachers make learning possible by first handling the babies' emotional vulnerability and then taking the time to observe them as they try out their knowledge and skills to see if what they know about the world holds true. Teachers make learning possible by being present to support infant engagement in this process. In this way, curiosity is stirred and discovery happens because the baby is emotionally ready for engagement. Yet rich cognitive learning can happen only when these new events are not stressful experiences. The infant care teacher needs to think of the emotional context needed for baby learning. A key way infant care teachers promote infant cognitive development is by being available to modulate infant states in response to novel experiences. They may have to use subtle gestures, facial expressions, touch, and their voice to help an infant calm down when the infant is emotionally aroused by a new experience or setting. In other cases, when an infant is not engaged in discovery, the infant may need the infant care teacher to stimulate positive emotional states and exhibit an intellectual curiosity of his or her own using the relationship to fuel the child's exploration of the novel environment (Raikes 1993, 1996; Raikes and Edwards 2009). The teacher who is attentive to the infant's process of discovery develops an understanding of the way the infant learns, knowing that different types of exchanges are a part of infant learning. During this process, infants connect both the cues and supports they receive from their teacher with the joy of discovery.

Skills that are crucial to success later in life, including the ability to inhibit one's urges (inhibition), the ability to hold some information in mind while attending to something else (working memory), and the ability to switch attention or mental focus (cognitive flexibility), are being developed and shaped through the give-and-take of relationships in which the baby is engaging during the first two years of life (Thompson 2009). The PITC defines being "in tune" as responding to emo-

tional and cognitive needs and reading babies' cues appropriately. Teachers who are "in tune" can do quite amazing things to help babies learn; through comforting interactions, these teachers can minimize an infant's negative states, and through interactive play they can stimulate both positive emotional states and intellectual curiosity (Raikes 1993, 1996; Raikes and Pope Edwards 2009). The context of a secure relationship with a caring adult who understands and respects both the baby's emotional vulnerability and intellectual competence is where meaningful learning takes place.

References

Belsky, J., B. Spritz, and K. Crnic. 1994. "Infant Attachment Security and Affective–Cognitive Information Processing at Age 3." *Psychological Science* 7 (2): 111–14.

Brothers, L. 1990. "The Social Brain: A Project for Integrating Primate Behavior and Neurophysiology in a New Domain." *Concepts in Neuroscience* 1:27–51.

Gopnik, A. 2009. "Your Baby Is Smarter Than You Think." *The New York Times*, August 16, WK10.

Gopnik, A., A. N. Meltzoff, and P. K. Kuhl. 1999. *The Scientist in the Crib: Minds, Brains, and How Children Learn*. Fairfield, NJ: William Morrow.

Greenspan, S. I. 1990. "Emotional Development in Infants and Toddlers." In *Infant/Toddler Caregiving: A Guide to Social–Emotional Growth and Socialization*, edited by J. R. Lally, 15–18. Sacramento: California Department of Education.

Honig, A. S. 2002. *Secure Relationships: Nurturing Infant/Toddler Attachment in Early Care Settings*. Washington, DC: National Association for the Education of Young Children.

National Research Council & Institute of Medicine. 2000. *From Neurons to Neighborhoods: The Science of Early Childhood Development*, edited by J. P. Shonkoff and D. A. Phillips, Board on Children, Youth, and Families; Commission on Behavioral and Social Sciences and Education. Washington, DC: National Academies Press.

Raikes, H. 1993. "Relationship Duration in Infant Care: Time with a High-Ability Teacher and Infant Teacher Attachment." *Early Childhood Research Quarterly* 8 (3): 309–25.

———. 1996. "A Secure Base for Babies: Applying Attachment Concepts to the Infant Care Settings." *Young Children* 51 (5): 59–67.

Raikes, H., and C. Pope Edwards. 2009. *Extending the Dance in Infant and Toddler Caregiving*. Baltimore: Brookes.

Schore, A. 2001. "The Effects of a Secure Attachment Relationship on Right Brain Development, Affect Regulation, and Infant Mental Health." *Infant Mental Health Journal* 22:7–66.

———. 2003. *Affect Dysregulation and Disorders of the Self*. New York: W. W. Norton.

———. 2005. "Attachment, Affect Regulation, and the Developing Right Brain: Linking Developmental Neuroscience to Pediatrics." *Pediatrics in Review* 26 (6): 204–17.

Siegel, D. 2001. "Toward an Interpersonal Neurobiology of the Developing Mind: Attachment Relationships, 'Mindsight,' and Neural Integration." *Infant Mental Health Journal* 22 (1–2): 67–94.

Sroufe, L. A. 1996. *Emotional Development*. Cambridge, England: Cambridge University Press.

Thompson, R. 2009. Doing What Doesn't Come Naturally. *Zero to Three Journal* 30 (2): 33–39.

Tronick, E. 2005. "Why Is Connection with Others So Critical? The Formation of Dyadic States of Consciousness: Coherence Governed Selection and the Co-creation of Meaning out of Messy Meaning Making." In *Emotional Development*, edited by J. Nadel and D. Muir, 293–315. New York: Oxford University Press.

Supporting Cognitive Development Through Interactions with Young Infants

Tiffany Field

Very young infants (from birth to six months of age) are fascinated by the world around them. They notice sights, sounds, smells, touches, and movements. When something catches their attention, they often want to find out more about it. If something happens once, they often enjoy seeing or hearing it happen again. Of greatest interest to them—what they want to learn most about—is their adult caregivers. Young infants focus intently on the actions of their caregivers. Facial expressions, smiles, sounds, touches, and gestures from the caregiver often delight them. Through innate responses, such as smiles, coos, and raised eyebrows, young infants communicate to their caregiver what interests them. Through playful

exchanges of such behaviors as coos, facial expressions, and smiles with an adult who understands their messages, they learn how to take turns and how to interact with a partner.

The intellectual development of young infants depends on their ability to organize their behavior for interaction with their caregivers. To help young infants organize their behavior, caregivers need to know how to determine when young infants are ready to interact and learn from social exchanges and how to adjust to each child's individual rhythm and style during interaction. This chapter begins with an overview of the importance of the young infants' social behaviors and biological rhythms in their development. The second part of the chapter focuses on responses and actions from the caregiver that enable very young infants to learn from social interaction.

Early Behaviors and Interaction

The young infant is capable of communicating to the caregiver through a host of signals. The primary means through which the infant communicates are looking behavior, facial expressions, vocalizations, and body movements.

Looking Behavior

During the early months of infancy, the primary skill of infants is *looking behavior.* Young infants can look at a person or thing, look away, close their eyes, and

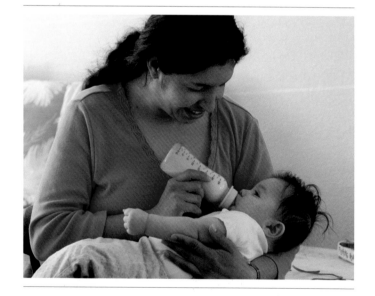

lating activity (touches, smiles, coos, and so forth) when the infant becomes inattentive or looks away. In effect, the infant is saying, "For right now, I've had enough cooing, smiling, laughing, and tickling. Give me some time to settle down." After a while, if the baby calms down and looks at you with bright eyes, he or she is saying, "I am ready for some action. Let's be playful."

Thus, gaze alternation, or looking at and looking away, is natural behavior that is affected by the type, amount, and timing of stimulation (Stern 1974). The infant (like the adult) needs periods of looking away to process the stimulation he or she received during the previous looking period or simply to calm down (Field 1981). When the adult fails to respect the infant's looking-away periods and interprets them as the infant's need for a break from conversation, the interaction becomes difficult or disturbed (Brazelton, Koslowski, and Main 1974; Field 1977a). With too much stimulation and no chance to settle down, a young baby can easily become overexcited and perhaps fussy. In such a state, the infant is no longer able to interact in an organized way.

Although looking at and looking away during interaction with the caregiver is typical behavior for young infants, some infants, at a very early stage, persistently avert their gaze (always look away) even with sensitive caregivers. In some cases, such avoidant behavior may be due to the infant's temperament. Some infants may react strongly to bright lights, noise, or touch; as a result, these infants may avoid

turn their heads. Looking behavior is the only system over which infants have a considerable degree of control and the only system that can be turned on or off. Caregivers spend virtually all of their one-to-one interaction time looking at the infant (Stern 1974). However, whether the infant looks at the caregiver's face seems to depend on the infant's state of alertness and the type of stimulation the caregiver is providing (Field 1977a). The young infant seems to look away from the caregiver's face to process the stimulation he or she is receiving.

Because the infant can use visual behavior to tune in and tune out of sources of stimulation, the infant's gazing (both looking at and looking away from the caregiver) becomes an important signal to the caregiver. The caregiver's reactions to an infant's gazing appear to play a critical role in engaging the infant in eye-to-eye contact. Consequently, T. Berry Brazelton and others (1974) have suggested that one of the most important skills for the caregiver to learn is sensitivity to the infant's capacity for attention and inattention. Being sensitive to a young baby's looking behavior means stopping stimu-

stimulation from caregivers. In addition, caregivers may have difficulty interacting with infants whose innate temperaments are characterized by low levels of alertness, cuddliness, consolability, or visual attentiveness. For more detailed information on temperament and its effects on interactions with infants, see "Temperaments of Infants and Toddlers," a chapter by Stella Chess, in *Infant/Toddler Caregiving: A Guide to Social–Emotional Growth and Socialization,* and the DVD *Flexible, Fearful, or Feisty: The Temperaments of Infants and Toddlers* (California Department of Education 1990).

Face, Voice, and Body

Infants' smiling and laughter are behaviors that delight caregivers. During early interactions such behaviors seldom occur spontaneously except when they are elicited by tickling or game playing (Sroufe and Wunsch 1972). A facial expression that occurs relatively often is the raised eyebrow, a kind of curiosity expression. The infant's pout-and-cry faces are very familiar to caregivers. Because these expressions often look quite adultlike, they are easy to interpret as signals of discontent. Pout-and-cry faces typically signal the end of a face-to face interaction. Similarly, crying, arching of the back, and general squirming typically precede the end of an interaction. Sometimes this behavior means that the infant is tired; sometimes, that the caregiver is overstimulating the child; and sometimes, that the infant is uncomfortable in the face-to-face position.

Activity Rhythms and Interaction

The very young infant's biological rhythms affect when the child is ready to interact with an adult; for example, from being awake to falling asleep, from being active to becoming inactive, and from being attentive to becoming inattentive. When preparing for interaction, the caregiver needs to give special attention to two aspects of biological rhythms: namely, the young infant's state of alertness and pauses in activity.

State of Alertness

An infant interacts best with a caregiver when the infant is awake and alert. At the beginning, the young infant moves from a sleeping state to an awake state frequently and stays awake for only short periods of time. During the next several weeks and months, the young infant becomes increasingly organized so that most of the sleep time is consolidated at nighttime, and periods of alertness become longer. The increasingly longer sleep–wake cycle is a biological rhythm consisting of several phases. Infants who are awake experience fluctuating periods of alertness; within those periods, infants

become attentive and inattentive. If the caregiver interacts with an infant who is awake but not fully alert or ready for interaction, the infant will often try to avoid the stimulation from the caregiver; or the infant may quickly become inattentive or even fussy. In contrast, by waiting for an optimal state of alertness, the caregiver can help the infant sustain attention or moments of alertness for interaction.

In general, as the infant learns to organize his or her various activity rhythms (for example, sucking, gaze alternations, and limb movements), interactions can become more prolonged. Caregivers can facilitate this development by being sensitive and adapting to the infant's rhythms and other signals of interaction and thereby support a rhythmic turn-taking interaction.

Pauses in Activity

Biological rhythms become more stabilized during the first few months; for example, sleep–awake periods become more prolonged (Thoman 1975). Yet infants and adults have to adjust continually to each other's rhythms. An example of this process of adjustment comes from a study of interactions between a caregiver and an infant during bottle-feeding. Adult stimulation was found to be typically reserved for pauses in the sucking activity or for times when the infant could interact freely because he or she was not preoccupied with sucking (Field 1977b).

Role of the Adult Partner

The caregiver's role in early learning is both multifaceted and quite special. Designing, maintaining, and changing the environment; keeping the daily schedule and the environment organized; and providing interesting stimulation are large tasks in themselves. On top of that list,

the caregiver needs to be a sensitive, responsive interaction partner who offers a variety of interesting games to the infant. Face-to-face interaction is extremely critical to the overall development of the very young infant, including the learning of early social skills, such as facial expressions and turn-taking.

Face-to-face interaction can take place when the infant is on the caregiver's lap, in an infant seat, or lying on his or her back on the floor. In any of these situations, the head of the caregiver should be lined up approximately with that of the infant at about 15 inches from the infant's face so that the infant can clearly see the caregiver's face. Being placed in a face-to-face position with the caregiver is typically popular with infants for at least the first eight months of life. After that age, the infant becomes more interested in manipulating objects and moving around while learning to crawl.

Simplify Behavior

Behaviors of adult caregivers are, of course, much more developed than the infant's. Much of what the caregiver needs to do has been described as "infantized" behavior (Field 1978).

Ways to simplify or infantize behavior include slowing down and exaggerating speech in a manner referred to as baby talk or "motherese" (Stern 1974). Facial expressions are also exaggerated, slowed down, and prolonged. When a caregiver interacts with a young infant, the sloweddown speech and exaggerated facial expressions help the infant to process or understand the caregiver's behaviors. Thus, when a caregiver infantizes behavior during interaction, the infant is better able to follow what the caregiver is doing and become more effective at turn taking.

Respond Contingently

As described by Bornstein in this guide, contingent responses occur within seconds of the infant's behavior and either meet the infant's communicated need or are similar to the infant's behavior. Several researchers have suggested that contingent or prompt responses similar to the infant's action are necessary so that the infant can feel that he or she has some influence on the interaction (Ainsworth and Bell 1974; Goldberg 1977; Lewis and Goldberg 1969; Watson 1967). If the caregiver's response is appropriate and given within a few seconds of the infant's behavior, the infant will more likely perceive that the caregiver's behavior is a direct response to his or her own behavior. Research studies have shown that adults view infant behaviors such as smiling, cooing, and eye-to-eye contact as posi-

tive responses. Such responses encourage adults to continue the game. For example, infants' smiling and vocalizing are frequently followed by similar behaviors from adults (Gewirtz and Gewirtz 1969; Lewis and Wilson 1972).

Imitate Behavior

Research studies have shown that a lot of caregiving behavior is imitative. Adults probably imitate the infant's behavior so that the infant may more easily understand his or her own behavior. Infants enjoy being imitated and are more able to imitate caregivers' imitations of their own behaviors (Field, Guy, and Umbel 1985). Thus, when interacting in a one-to-one situation with an infant, caregivers typically imitate the most frequently occurring infant behaviors—for example, grimaces more than laughter in the very young infant and laughter more than grimaces in the slightly older infant. Very soon after birth, infants are able to imitate simple behaviors such as sticking out their tongues and making happy, sad, and surprised faces (Field and others 1982; Meltzoff and Moore 1977).

Repeat a Behavior

Repetition of actions is another way to help infants understand the interaction partner more easily. Repetition gives the infant multiple opportunities to connect his or her actions with those of the adult.

Highlight a Behavior

A frequent behavior of caregivers is called "highlighting" of the infant's behaviors. Caregivers frequently give a running commentary or describe and label aloud the infant's behaviors as they happen. For example, if the infant has hiccups, the caregiver will say, "Oh, you have the hiccups" or "Sweet baby, you always spit up when you get happy."

Play Games

Caregivers also play a number of games that have been observed around the world and labeled infant games. They include Peek-a-boo, So Big, Tell Me a Story, Crawling, Itsy-Bitsy Spider, and Pat-a-cake (Field 1979). These games invariably lead to smiling and laughter from the infant but should be played when the child is at the appropriate age. When a caregiver tries to play age-inappropriate games (for example, playing Pat-a-cake with a six-week-old rather than with a three-month-old infant), the interaction will be disrupted. A six-week-old infant will be unable to follow a game such as Pat-a-cake and may become upset or inattentive if the caregiver initiates such a game. In contrast, the typical three-month-old infant will be able to follow the caregiver's movements during Pat-a-cake and will usually remain attentive and enjoy the game. Sensitivity to the baby's signals will help the caregiver to know whether a game is appropriate or inappropriate for an infant. Infants' games also provide opportunities for turn taking or responsive give-and-take with an infant. One of the most popular games of the young infant is Tell Me a Story. The words are provided by the caregiver, who treats the infant's vocalizations as if they, too, are words. For instance, in playing the game, the caregiver asks, "Do you want to tell me a story?" The infant coos; the adult responds, "Oh, yeah? And then what happened?" The infant coos again, and the adult replies, "Oh, that's funny." The infant smiles, coos, and sometimes laughs; and the caregiver then responds by playing more of the same game. When the infant no longer responds contentedly to the game, it is a signal to move on to still another game or "conversation" or perhaps to give the child a chance to become organized for more interaction, have private time, or take a rest.

Summary

The very young infant's development in general and intellectual development in particular depend on a caregiver who:

- waits until the infant is in a quiet, attentive state of alertness before interacting with the infant;

- responds promptly when the child expresses an interest or need;

- "infantizes" or slows down, exaggerates, and repeats behaviors;

- responds by imitating or highlighting the infant's behaviors;

- takes turns and does not interrupt the infant;

- plays games that are interesting and age-appropriate; and

- respects the infant's occasional breaks from the interaction.

Becoming a sensitive interaction partner makes caregiving fun because the infant enjoys and appreciates such care. At the same time, sensitive and responsive caregiving provides the infant with the experiences he or she needs to understand and learn about the world.

References

Ainsworth, M. D. S., and S. M. Bell. 1974. "Mother–Infant Interaction and the Development of Competence." In *The Growth of Competence*, edited by K. J. Connolly and J. S. Bruner. New York: Academic Press.

Brazelton, T. B., B. Koslowski, and M. Main. 1974. "The Origins of Reciprocity: The Early Mother–Infant Interaction." In *The Effect of the Infant on Its Caregiver*, edited by M. Lewis and L. Rosenblum. New York: John Wiley and Sons.

California Department of Education. 1990. *Flexible, Fearful, or Feisty: The Different Temperaments of Infants and Toddlers*. Sacramento: California Department of Education. DVD, 29 minutes.

Field, T. 1977a. "Effects of Early Separation, Interactive Deficits, and Experimental Manipulations on Infant–Mother Face-to-Face Interaction." *Child Development* 48 (3): 763–71.

———. 1977b. "Maternal Stimulation During Infant Feeding." *Developmental Psychology* 13 (5): 539–40.

———. 1978. "The Three Rs of Infant Adult Interactions: Rhythms, Repertoires, and Responsivity." *Journal of Pediatric Psychology* 3:131–36.

———. 1979. "Games Parents Play with Normal and High-Risk Infants." *Child Psychiatry and Human Development* 10:41–48.

———. 1981. "Gaze Behavior of Normal and High-Risk Infants During Early Interactions." *Journal of the American Academy of Child Psychiatry* 20:308–17.

Field, T., L. Guy, and V. Umbel. 1985. "Infants' Responses to Mothers' Imitative Behaviors." *Infant Mental Health Journal* 6:40–44.

Field, T., R. Woodson, R. Greenburg, and D. Cohen. 1982. "Discrimination and Imitation of Facial Expressions by Neonates." *Science* 218 (4568): 179–81.

Gewirtz, H. B., and J. L. Gewirtz. 1969. "Caretaking Settings, Background Events, and Behavior Differences in Four Israeli Child Rearing Environments: Some Preliminary Trends." In *Determinants of Infant Behavior*, edited by B. Foss, vol. 4. London: Methuen.

Goldberg, S. 1977. "Social Competence in Infancy: A Model of Parent–Infant Interaction." *Merrill-Palmer Quarterly* 23 (3): 163–77.

Lewis, M., and S. Goldberg. 1969. "Perceptual–Cognitive Development in Infancy: A Generalized Expectancy

Model as a Function of the Mother Infant Interaction." *Merrill-Palmer Quarterly* 15 (1): 81–100.

Lewis, M., and C. D. Wilson. 1972. "Infant Development in Lower-Class American Families." *Human Development* 15:112–27.

Meltzoff, A. N., and M. K. Moore. 1977. "Imitation of Facial and Manual Gestures by Human Neonates." *Science* 198 (4312, October 7): 75–78.

Sroufe, L. A., and J. P. Wunsch. 1972. "The Development of Laughter in the First Year of Life." *Child Development* 43 (4): 1326–44.

Stern, D. N. 1974. "Mother and Infant at Play: The Dyadic Interaction Involving Facial, Vocal, and Gaze Behaviors." In *The Effect of the Infant on Its Caregiver*, edited by M. Lewis and L. A. Rosenblum. New York: John Wiley and Sons.

Thoman, E. B. 1975. "Early Development of Sleeping Behaviors in Infants." In *Studies in Mother–Infant Interaction*, edited by H. R. Schaffer. London: Academic Press.

Watson, J. S. 1967. "Memory and 'Contingency Analysis' in Infant Learning." *Merrill-Palmer Quarterly* 13:55–76.

Section Two:

Culture and Cognitive
Development

The Connection between Culture and Cognitive Development

Lucía Alcalá and Barbara Rogoff

Children learn and develop by expanding on what they already know, building on their prior knowledge (Bransford, Brown, and Cocking 1999). One of the most important sources of children's prior knowledge is their cultural experience (Rogoff 2003; Vygotsky 1978). Infants and young children learn from their day-to-day activities with other people in cultural communities that promote practices that are often supported by the members of families and communities (Whiting and Whiting 1975).

Communities are organized in ways that give young children access to certain activities and not to others. As a result, children are likely to know how to engage in activities that they experience in their communities. For example, if children have the opportunity to ride along in canoes and to maneuver a small canoe, they may learn to do so at an early age (Wilbert 1979). If the households of a community have an open fireplace for cooking, children may be discouraged from crawling and may be slower to learn to crawl—but not necessarily slower to learn to walk (Hewlett 1991). If children never experience stairs, they may initially have difficulty with them (Super 1981).

As we live our lives, we develop familiar repertoires of cultural practices through our immersion in everyday events and routines of the varied communities in which we participate. Taking part in these events and routines allows us to develop a wide range of cognitive skills, such as ways for understanding the physical and social world, learning

abstract concepts, knowing subtle rules of communication, understanding number systems, and learning how to adjust our approaches to different situations.

To understand the cognitive abilities of infants and children, we need to consider cultural variation in children's experience with different cultural practices—their repertoires of cultural practices—because any particular situation may call for different approaches depending on children's cultural experience. For example, determining whether an infant realizes that objects continue to exist even if they go out of sight (Piaget's concept of object permanence) involves practices that may hold different meaning for children from various cultural backgrounds. If an adult jingles keys in front of a baby and then hides them under a cloth, and the baby reaches for the hidden keys, the adult may conclude that a child has object permanence. However, in a Mayan town in Guatemala, infants often might not reach for the attractive object under such circumstances. But it would be risky to conclude that children lack a sense of object permanence—if even very young children learn a form of consideration that precludes grabbing other people's things (such as the keys). So if infants do not reach for the keys, we cannot conclude that it is because they lack object permanence. Within their repertoire of practice, the situation may call for politely *not* grabbing the keys.

Children's repertoires of practice expand rapidly within the first few years of life. Infants and young children learn many skills, values, beliefs, and expectations of their communities even before the age of two. As they have the opportunities to become involved in new activities, they can learn the practices of other communities as well. Ideally, these would amplify their repertoires of practices, not replace what they already know and do.

In this chapter we examine important cultural differences in young children's ways of attending to what is going on around them, their skills in contributing to community activities and participating in particular forms of adult–child interaction, their knowledge of how aspects of the world work, and their flexibility in adapting their skills and knowledge in to specific situations.

Developing Keen Attention to Surrounding Events

One important way that infants' and young children's cognitive development relates to their cultural experience is the development of keen attention to surrounding events. Keen attention is a critical aspect of infants' cognitive development; they learn a vast amount of information by observing others around them (Akhtar 2005; Rogoff 2003).

Cultural differences in attention show up among infants and toddlers. Guatemalan Mayan toddlers (like their mothers) were found to be more likely to pay attention to surrounding events than were middle-class European American toddlers (and their mothers), who tended to pay attention more narrowly (Chavajay and Rogoff 1999; Rogoff et al. 1993). For example, one Mayan twelve-month-old was so alert that he skillfully and simultaneously paid attention to his mother's request to blow on a whistle, his sister's help with a toy he was handling, and a truck that was passing by. Similarly, three- to five-year-old Mayan children tended to be alert to the activities of their mothers and younger siblings and other nearby events, whereas middle-class European American children tended to pay attention only to their own activities (Silva, Shimpi, and Rogoff 2009). Relatedly, among middle-class European American infants, joint visual attention does not reliably appear until about eight to ten months of age (Corkum and Moore 1998), but Mexican Mayan infants as young as six months were reported to orient their gaze together with their caregiver when they heard the caregiver greet a neighbor passing by, participating in greeting interactions with skilled attention and growing awareness of others' intentions (de Leon 2000). In this community and other indigenous communities of the Americas, young children seem to be especially inclined to attend skillfully to ongoing events (Gaskins 1999; Magazine and Ramírez Sánchez 2007).

Where might such cultural differences in keen attentiveness to ongoing events come from? These young children's daily lives differ in ways that are likely to promote different approaches to paying attention. The Mayan infants and children mentioned before were included in a wide range of activities of their families and communities, and they were expected to pay attention and begin to help out as they became able. For example,

Guatemalan Mayan three-year-olds were more often in the presence of adult work, with the opportunity to observe, than were middle-class European American three-year-olds (Morelli, Rogoff, and Angelillo 2003). Mayan parents emphasized to young children to be observant in everyday activities and expected them to learn through observation. It was not uncommon for parents to scold children for missing something the children could have seen: "What are your eyes for?" (Chavajay 1993, 165).

In contrast, middle-class European American children spent more of their time segregated from the range of community activities and often focused their attention more narrowly (Morelli, Rogoff, and Angelillo 2003; Rogoff et al. 1993). In many family and child care settings, and eventually in schools, middle-class European American children's attention is often managed by adults (Paradise et al. 2007). Adults may urge them not to pay attention to surrounding events, requiring them to just pay attention to what the children themselves or the adult is doing, such as by calling out "One, two, three; eyes on me" and requiring children to respond "One, two; eyes on you."

Thus very young children of differing backgrounds have the opportunity to learn very different preferences for attention. Infants and toddlers seem to already have learned the distinct patterns of their communities.

Developing Skills for Everyday Community Life and for Child-Directed Situations

Differences in young children's everyday skills are associated with children's inclusion in the range of activities of their community or segregation into settings designed for children. Their learning is channeled by opportunities to observe and engage in different activities and by the attitudes of those around them. Children learn situationally valued ways to solve problems, interact, and approach new situations. The differences in skills may be related to distinct views of what young children are capable of.

Early childhood in some communities, such as in indigenous communities of the Americas, is seen as a period of productive contributions to the family and community. In such communities, infants and young children are considered community members from the day of their birth, even if they are not yet making real contributions to their community (Ramírez Sánchez 2007). They are included in work, ceremonial events, social events, church, and other community events (Corona and Perez 2007; Rogoff 2003). During these activities, children can learn important cognitive skills, and their contributions to family work are formative for them (Alcalá et al. 2009; Magazine and Ramírez Sánchez 2007).

In communities where infants are seldom included in community events, adults often create child-specialized settings that provide infants and young children with particular toys and activities. Young children are often restricted to certain areas, limiting their mobility and access to adults' activities for protection of the children as well as of adults' activities, rather than treated as capable of engaging in the broader activities of the community. When they are involved in social interaction, infants and toddlers are often spoken to in a specialized one-on-one, face-to-face model with simplified baby talk (Ochs and Schieffelin 1984).

Children whose days are spent in child-specialized activities learn to engage in child-specialized activities. For example, these toddlers learn how to take their part in interactions designed by adults to elicit talk, such as games labeling body parts: "Where is your belly button?" These forms of interaction are not actual requests for information about where the body part is, but games that are specialized for infants and young children.

Participating in such known-answer questions closely resembles the kind of quizzing that often happens in preschool and school, such as "What color is this?" or "How many legs does a spider have?" Differing levels of familiarity with the routines used in testing may be an important basis of the school "achievement gap" across ethnic groups in the United States. Young children who are familiar with known-answer questions can engage with little trouble, but when those who have little such experience first encounter such forms of interaction, they may be puzzled and have difficulty knowing how to respond. Similarly, young children may be interrupted and criticized by teachers during "sharing time" if the teachers are unfamiliar with the valued structure of narrative in children's home communities (Michaels 1981). But, of course, with some experience and assistance, children can learn how to take part in new situations (and adults can learn about cultural practices that are new to them).

Children who have little experience in situations that are designed by adults for young children often have other experiences that promote other skills. If they are included as contributors to a wide range of community activities, they have the opportunity to become quite skilled in the activities of importance that surround them.

Extensive research documents the skills of young children in many parts of the world to contribute to their family's activities. By age three, a child may be able to care for a younger child (under supervision), cook a meal on a fire, sweep the house, run errands, and take produce they have grown themselves to the market to sell, contributing to the family income (Hewlett 1991; Rogoff 2003; Watson-Gegeo 1990; Whiting and Edwards 1988). For example, three-year-old children in Japan help change and feed infants, take toddlers to the restroom, help them go up or down the stairs, and carry them to the playground, "adopting" a younger child as their special charge and visiting the nursery several times during the day to help (Tobin, Wu, and Davidson 1989).

If children have the opportunity to be included in both school-like and household/community activities, their repertoire of practices can expand to include both the skills that are commonplace in schooling and those that are valued in household and community events. For example, Bella, a two-year-old girl of Mexican heritage, has been included since birth in a range of academic activities as her mother, a graduate researcher, brought Bella to many academic activities such as lab meetings, lectures, and professional conferences. Bella knows how to sit quietly and listen when others are doing so and when it is appropriate to chat. From her first year of life, she "took notes," scribbling as others wrote. When she was eight months old, Bella picked up a pen from the floor during a graduate seminar and started "writing" in her mother's notebook.

At the same time, having the opportunity to help at home and be around extended family members has allowed Bella to develop other skills and knowledge.

Bella is always around her parents when they do chores around the house. By helping out with activities such as picking up trash, sorting laundry, and preparing meals, this two-year-old has learned, for example, the colors of the rainbow and to count to 10. She has also learned important self-care skills as well as a sense of responsibility from her family's and community's practice of allowing young children to contribute to ongoing activities.

One day, after playing with sand, Bella noticed that her hands were dirty and decided to go wash them. When she was done washing her hands, she noticed that her shirt was wet and dirty, so she took off her shirt and started to wash it in the bathroom sink. Because water spilled on the floor, she got the mop and started cleaning the floor. At that point, her socks got wet from the water that had spilled and so she decided to wash her socks too.

General Knowledge of Events

From their participation in daily activities, children create general knowledge about how the world works (Hudson, Shapiro, and Sosa 1995). Routine activities serve as contexts for developing a cognitive understanding of the structure of events, such as what is involved in going to a restaurant, milking a cow, tending a baby, going to school, or doing adult work. For example, toddlers in the United States whose parents worked at home had the opportunity to observe, showed understanding of their parents' work, and started to contribute to the work with simple and then more complex tasks (Beach 1988). Similarly, middle-class European American toddlers who helped adults in household tasks sometimes started before the parent began, showing an understanding of the goal of the activity and often carrying out appropriate actions that were not modeled by the adults in that moment (Rheingold 1982). Likewise, Bella, by being part of the daily activities at home, learned the sequence of events that usually take place when something is dirty and the steps needed to fix that problem. Young children who have the chance to help younger children may show the same sort of understanding of skills and even an understanding of others' intentions and mental states that is expected of older children in communities where children have little contact with and responsibility for younger children (Rogoff 2003). Thus children's cultural experience gives them understanding of how the world works.

It is sometimes difficult to consider the different background experiences of children when differences are noticed in their knowledge. It is easy to assume that unfamiliarity with knowledge familiar to everyone is an indicator of lack of intelligence. Instead, unfamiliarity should be interpreted in terms of a child's background experience. For example, a little girl who was unfamiliar with soft drinks before the age of three, because her parents tried to prevent her from gaining this knowledge, might be seen as ignorant if an observer did not know the child's background experience. On the other hand, the same child had learned unusual medical names of body parts by playing the Where Is Your Belly Button? game—to be funny, her parents included unusual body parts in the game, such as the *popliteal fossa* (the space at the back of the knee). When this toddler told her pediatrician that her popliteal fossa was itchy, the doctor was unduly impressed.

These individual examples underline the importance of taking children's background experience into account. Cultural differences in children's background experience are more crucial and difficult to consider. Flexibility in interpreting different cultural ways of learning and knowing is essential in caring for children of diverse cultural backgrounds. In fact, another key cognitive skill—flexibility in adaptation of skills and approaches according to different situations—is important for infant/toddler care teachers' as well as infants' and young children's learning.

Learning to Adjust to the Situation

Young children have the ability to expand their repertoire of practice as they participate in new situations. In addition, they need to learn how to fit their skills to the circumstances, and they are good at doing it. For example, infants and children who grow up in bilingual households learn quickly to switch from one communication system to the other, depending on the circumstances, such as which parent they are talking to and whether the children are at home or at school. They can also learn when to attend widely or focus narrowly, when to use their everyday skills related to school or to use their

skills related to responsible contributions in their family, which aspect of their general knowledge of events is relevant to the present situation, and many other cognitive approaches.

When to use which approach is a complex cognitive skill and is one of the most important cognitive skills for children to develop. Adults in some communities help children learn to distinguish which approach to use in which circumstance. For example, Japanese preschool teachers and mothers help young children notice the boundaries between ways of doing things at home versus at school (Ben-Ari 1996; Lebra 1994).

Adapting Care to Children's Cultural Experiences

Developing flexible repertoires of practices is also key for adults who care for children of different backgrounds. Teachers and caregivers in the United States are commonly taught about cultural styles of learning that are presented as rigid stereotypical categories. Sometimes teachers are encouraged to treat children of one background in one way and children of another background in another way, based on presumed cultural styles. For example, people from some backgrounds are regarded as more likely to collaborate or more likely to learn holistically, rather than analytically. But the idea of "cultural styles" can be restrictive if we do not recognize that young children, as well as adults, can expand their repertoires of practice and learn new ways (Gutiérrez and Rogoff 2003).

Focusing on people's repertoires of practice is a more open, flexible approach. Although people with various cultural experiences are likely to differ in what they know and how they prefer to do things, their knowledge and ways of doing things are not built into their ethnicity, race, or national background. Adults using an open-minded approach—trying to understand people's likely practices without pigeonholing people into static categories—can help children expand beyond practices of the home and know which approach is appropriate for a particular setting.

If different cultural practices are seen as incompatible, this juxtaposition in children's lives may result in a mismatch of practices—between the ways things are done at home and at school. An unfortunate result of treating different cultural practices as incompatible, rather than viewing them simply as different ways that can be part of a repertoire, is that children may be forced to choose between their home practices and school practices. Delgado-Gaitan (1990, 63) reported that "As Spanish-speaking children moved up the academic ladder and learned more English, parents were distanced from them and the schooling process. Some parents reported that by the time the child reached junior high school, they felt as if they were 'living with a stranger.'"

Infant/toddler care teachers who are alert to the potential for differences among young children based on the children's cultural experiences can be helpful by flexibly guiding young children (not pigeonholing or judging them) when introducing the children to new experiences. These infant/toddler care teachers realize that what feels "natural" may simply reflect their own more familiar way of doing things. They can help children learn new practices in addition to the cultural practices that the children are already familiar with from their homes.

It would be ideal if an infant/toddler care teacher could understand all the cultural practices that the children they care for are familiar with. But teachers are

already overburdened with responsibilities, and learning about cultural practices is a long process. In the meantime, teachers can make progress in understanding different cultural ways of the children they serve by having an open mind and an interest in learning.

A good way for infant/toddler care teachers to learn more is to consult with children's family members to better understand the children's cultural experience. If teachers focus on children's actual life experiences rather than children's ancestry, teachers may gain insights into fostering children's learning and development. Teachers can try to find some regularities in communities' ways of doing things while treating ideas about cultural practices in a community as only guesses about students' familiar practices. Then teachers can look, with an open mind, to see whether particular individuals have experience with the practices common in the cultural communities suggested by their ethnicity or race or community (Gutiérrez and Rogoff 2003). Such an open attitude allows teachers to learn more about the repertoires of practice that cultural groups or individual students have developed in their lives. Infant/toddler care teachers can learn about different repertoires of practice along with the children and families—not to "educate" families as if they were ignorant, but rather to recognize them as contributors and collaborators in the development of their children.

Infant/toddler care teachers can expand their own repertoire of practices as they help children expand their repertoire to successfully navigate through life. Openness to the idea that children can be taught, develop, and learn effectively in more than one way allows teachers to learn ways that are different from their own. This openness can lead to expanded repertoires of practices for both teachers and the young children in their care.

References

Akhtar, N. 2005. "The Robustness of Learning through Overhearing." *Developmental Science* 8 (2): 199–209.

Alcalá, L., R. Mejía-Arauz, B. Rogoff, and A. L. D. Roberts. 2009. "Children's Participation in Household Work and Child-Focused Activities." American Educational Research Association, April, San Diego.

Beach, B. A. 1988. "Children at Work: The Home Workplace." *Early Childhood Research Quarterly* 3:209–221.

Ben-Ari, E. 1996. "From Mothering to Othering: Organization, Culture, and Nap Time in a Japanese Day-Care Center." *Ethos* 24:136–64.

Bransford, J., A. L. Brown, and R. R. Cocking, eds. 1999. *How People Learn.* Washington, DC: National Academies Press.

Chavajay, P. 1993. "Independent Analyses of Cultural Variations and Similarities in San Pedro and Salt Lake." *Monographs of the Society for Research in Child Development* 58 (8): 162–65.

Chavajay, P., and B. Rogoff. 1999. "Cultural Variation in Management of Attention by Children and Their Caregivers." *Developmental Psychology* 35:1079–91.

———. 2002. "Schooling and Traditional Collaborative Social Organization of Problem Solving by Mayan Mothers and Children." *Developmental Psychology* 38:55–66.

Corkum, V., and C. Moore. 1998. "The Origins of Joint Visual Attention in Infants." *Developmental Psychology* 34:28–38.

Corona, Y., and C. Pérez. 2007. "The Importance of Child Participation in the Ritual Life for the Recreation of the Culture of the Indigenous Peoples." In *The Given Child: The Religions' Contributions to Children's Citizenship,* edited by T. Wyller and U. S. Nayar, 125–28.

Correa-Chávez, M., B. Rogoff, and R. Mejía-Arauz. 2005. "Cultural Patterns in Attending to Two Events at Once." *Child Development* 76:664–78.

de Leon, L. 2000. "The Emergent Participant: Interactive Patterns in the Socialization of Tzotzil (Mayan) Infants." *Journal of Linguistic Anthropology* 8:131–61.

Delgado-Gaitan, C. 1990. *Literacy for Empowerment.* London: Falmer.

———. 1994. "Socializing Young Children in Mexican-American Families."

In *Cross-Cultural Roots of Minority Child Development*, edited by P. M. Greenfield and R. R. Cocking, 55–86. Hillsdale, NJ: Erlbaum.

Gaskins, S. 1999. "Children's Daily Lives in a Mayan Village: A Case Study of Culturally Constructed Roles and Activities." In *Children's Engagement in the World: Sociocultural Perspectives,* edited by A. Göncu, 25–61. New York: Cambridge University Press.

Gutiérrez, K., and B. Rogoff. 2003. "Cultural Ways of Learning: Individual Traits or Repertoires of Practice." *Educational Researcher* 32:19–25.

Hewlett, B. S. 1991. *Intimate Fathers: The Nature and Context of Aka Pygmy Paternal Infant Care.* Ann Arbor: University of Michigan Press.

Hudson, J. A., L. R. Shapiro, and B. B. Sosa. 1995. "Planning in the Real World: Preschool Children's Scripts and Plans for Familiar Events." *Child Development* 66:984–98.

Lebra, T. S. 1994. "Mother and Child in Japanese Socialization: A Japan–U.S. Comparison." In *Cross-Cultural Roots of Minority Child Development,* edited by P. M. Greenfield and R. R. Cocking, 259–74. Hillsdale, NJ: Erlbaum.

Magazine, R., and M. A. Ramírez Sánchez. 2007. "Continuity and Changes in San Pedro Tlalcuapan, Mexico." In *Generations and Globalization,* edited by J. Cole and D. Durham, 52–73. Bloomington, IN: Indiana University Press.

Mejía-Arauz, R., B. Rogoff, A. L. Dexter, and B. Najafi. 2007. "Cultural Variation in Children's Social Organization." *Child Development* 78:1001–14.

Mejía-Arauz, R., B. Rogoff, and R. Paradise. 2005. "Cultural Variation in Children's Observation During a Demonstration." *International Journal of Behavioral Development* 29:282–91.

Michaels, S. 1981. "'Sharing Time': Children's Narrative Styles and Differential Access to Literacy." *Language in Society* 10:432–42.

Morelli, G., B. Rogoff, and C. Angelillo. 2003. "Cultural Variation in Children's Access to Work or Involvement in Specialized Child-Focused Activities. *International Journal of Behavioral Development* 27:264–74.

Ochs, E., and B. B. Schieffelin. 1984. "Language Acquisition and Socialization: Three Developmental Stories and Their Implications." In *Culture and Its Acquisition,* edited by R. Schweder and R. LeVine. Chicago: University of Chicago Press.

Paradise, R., R. Mejía Arauz, K. Silva, A. L. D. Roberts, and B. Rogoff. 2007. "Managing Others' Learning: Teacher Ways or Showing How." XXXI Congreso Interamericano de Psicología, Mexico City, July.

Ramírez Sánchez, M. A. 2007. "'Helping at Home': The Concept of Childhood and Work Among the Nahuas of Tlaxcala, Mexico." In *Working to Be Someone,* edited by B. Hungerland, M. Liebel, B. Milne, and A. Wihstutz, 87–95. London: Jessica Kingsley Publishers.

Rheingold, H. L. 1982. "Little Children's Participation in the Work of Adults." *Child Development* 53:114–25.

Rogoff, B. 2003. *The Cultural Nature of Human Development*. New York: Oxford.

Rogoff, B., M. Correa-Chávez, and K. G. Silva. 2011. "Cultural Variation in Children's Attention and Learning." In *Psychology and the Real World,* edited by M. A. Gernsbacher, R. W. Pew, L. Hough, and J. R. Pomerantz. New York: Worth.

Rogoff, B., J. J. Mistry, A. Göncü, and C. Mosier. 1993. "Guided Participation in Cultural Activity by Toddlers and Caregivers." *Monographs of the Society for Research in Child Development* 58 (7, Serial No. 236).

Silva, K. G., P. M. Shimpi, and B. Rogoff. 2009. "Children's Third-Party Attention to Naturalistic Interactions: A Mayan and European American Comparison." Unpublished article under review.

Super, C. M. 1981. "Behavioral Development in Infancy." In *Handbook of Cross-Cultural Human Development,* edited by R. H. Munroe, R. L. Munroe, and B. B. Whiting. New York: Garland.

Tobin, J. J., D. Y. H. Wu, and D. H. Davidson. 1989. *Preschool in Three Cultures*. New Haven: Yale University Press.

Vygotsky, L. S. 1978. *Mind in Society.* Cambridge, MA: Harvard University Press.

Watson-Gegeo, K. A. 1990. "The Social Transfer of Cognitive Skills in Kwara'ae." *Quarterly Newsletter of the Laboratory of Comparative Human Cognition* 12:86–90.

Whiting, B. B., and C. P. Edwards. 1988. *Children of Different Worlds*. Cambridge, MA: Harvard University Press.

Whiting, B. B., and J. W. M. Whiting. 1975. *Children of Six Cultures*. Cambridge, MA: Harvard.

Wilbert, J. 1979. "To Become a Maker of Canoes: An Essay on Warao Enculturation." In *Enculturation in Latin America*. UCLA Latin America Center Publications. Los Angeles: University of California.

Appendix

Appendix

Cognitive Development

"The last two decades of infancy research have seen dramatic changes in the way developmental psychologists characterize the earliest stages of cognitive development. The infant, once regarded as an organism driven mainly by simple sensorimotor schemes, is now seen as possessing sophisticated cognitive skills and even sophisticated concepts that guide knowledge acquisition" (Madole and Oakes 1999, 263).

"What we see in the crib is the greatest mind that has ever existed, the most powerful learning machine in the universe" (Gopnik, Meltzoff, and Kuhl 1999, 1).

The term *cognitive development* refers to the process of growth and change in intellectual/mental abilities such as thinking, reasoning and understanding. It includes the acquisition and consolidation of knowledge. Infants draw on social-emotional, language, motor, and perceptual experiences and abilities for cognitive development. They are attuned to relationships between features of objects, actions, and the physical environment. But they are particularly attuned to people. Parents, family members, friends, teachers, and caregivers play a vital role in supporting the cognitive development of infants by providing the healthy interpersonal or social-emotional context in which cognitive development unfolds.

Note: Reprinted from the *California Infant/Toddler Learning & Development Foundations,* pages 59–86, with permission from the California Department of Education.

Caring, responsive adults provide the base from which infants can fully engage in behaviors and interactions that promote learning. Such adults also serve as a prime source of imitation.

Cultural context is important to young children's cognitive development. There is substantial variation in how intelligence is defined within different cultures (Sternberg and Grigorenko 2004). As a result, different aspects of cognitive functioning or cognitive performance may be more highly valued in some cultural contexts than in others. For example, whereas processing speed is an aspect of intelligence that is highly valued within the predominant Western conceptualizations of intelligence, "Ugandan villagers associate intelligence with adjectives such as slow, careful, and active" (Rogoff and Chavajay 1995, 865.). Aspects of intelligence that have to do with social competence appear to be seen as more important than speed in some non-Western cultural contexts (Sternberg and Grigorenko 2004). Certainly, it is crucial for early childhood professionals to recognize the role that cultural context plays in defining and setting the stage for children's healthy cognitive functioning.

Research has identified a broad range of cognitive competencies and described the remarkable progression of cognitive development during the early childhood years. Experts in the field describe infants as active, motivated, and engaged learners who possess an impressive range of cognitive competencies (National Research Council and Institute of Medicine 2000) and learn through exploration (Whitehurst and Lonigan 1998). Infants demonstrate natural curiosity. They have a strong drive to learn and act accordingly. In fact, they have been described as "born to learn" (National Research Council and Institute of Medicine 2000, 148).

Cause-and-Effect

Everyday experiences—for example, crying and then being picked up or waving a toy and then hearing it rattle—provide opportunities for infants to learn about cause and effect. "Even very young infants possess expectations about physical events" (Baillargeon 2004, 89). This knowledge helps infants better understand the properties of objects, the patterns of human behavior, and the relationship between events and the consequences. Through developing an understanding of cause and effect, infants build their abilities to solve problems, to make predictions, and to understand the impact of their behavior on others.

Spatial Relationships

Infants learn about spatial relationships in a variety of ways; for example, exploring objects with their mouths, tracking objects and people visually, squeezing into tight spaces, fitting objects into openings, and looking at things from different perspectives (Mangione, Lally, and Signer 1992). They spend much of their time exploring the physical and spatial aspects of the environment, including the characteristics of, and interrelationships between, the people, objects, and the physical space around them (Clements 2004). The development of an understanding of spatial relationships increases infants' knowledge of how things move and fit in space and the properties of objects (their bodies and the physical environment).

Problem Solving

Infants exhibit a high level of interest in solving problems. Even very young infants will work to solve a problem, for example, how to find their fingers in order to suck on them (National Research Council and Institute of Medicine 2000). Older infants may solve the problem of how to reach an interesting toy that is out of reach by trying to roll toward it or by gesturing to an adult for help. Infants and toddlers solve problems by varied means, including physically acting on objects, using learning schemes they have developed, imitating solutions found by others, using objects or other people as tools, and using trial and error.

Imitation

Imitation is broadly understood to be a powerful way to learn. It has been identified as crucial in the acquisition of cultural knowledge (Rogoff 1990) and language. Imitation by newborns has been demonstrated for adult facial expressions (Meltzoff and Moore 1983), head movements, and tongue protrusions (Meltzoff and Moore 1989). "The findings of imitation in human newborns highlighted predispositions to imitate facial and manual actions, vocalizations and emotionally laden facial expressions" (Bard and Russell 1999, 93). Infant imitation involves perception and motor processes (Meltzoff and Moore 1999). The very early capacity to imitate makes possible imitation games in which the adult mirrors the child's behavior, such as sticking out one's tongue or matching the pitch of a sound the infant makes, and then the infant imitates back. This type of interaction builds over time as the infant and the adult add elements and variations in their imitation games.

Infants engage in both immediate imitation and delayed imitation. Immediate imitation occurs when infants observe and immediately attempt to copy or mimic behavior. For example, immediate imitation can be seen when an infant's parent sticks out his tongue and the infant sticks out his tongue in response. As infants develop, they are able to engage in delayed imitation, repeating the behavior of others at a later time after having observed it. An example of delayed imitation is a child reenacting part of a parent's exercise routine, such as lifting a block several times as if it were a weight. Butterworth (1999, 63) sums up the importance of early imitation in the following manner: "Modern research has shown imitation to be a natural mechanism of learning and communication which deserves to be at centre stage in developmental psychology."

Memory

The capacity to remember allows infants and toddlers to differentiate between familiar and unfamiliar people and objects, anticipate and participate in parts of personal care routines, learn language, and come to know the rules of social interaction. The infant's memory system is quite remarkable and functions at a higher level than was previously believed (Howe and Courage 1993). Although age is not the only determinant of memory functioning, as infants get older they are able to retain information for longer periods of time (Bauer 2004). Infants exhibit long-term recall well before they are able to articulate their past experiences verbally (Bauer 2002b).

The emergence of memory is related to the development of a neural network with various components (Bauer 2002b).

Commenting on the different forms and functions of early memory development, Bauer (2002a, 131) states: "It is widely believed that memory is not a unitary trait but is comprised of different systems or processes, which serve distinct functions, and are characterized by fundamentally different rules of operation." Bauer (2002a, 145) later adds that recent research counters earlier suggestions that preschool-aged children demonstrate little memory capacity and to speculations that younger children and infants demonstrate little or no memory capacity. Bauer (2002a, 145) concludes: "It is now clear that from early in life, the human organism stores information over the long term and that the effects of prior experience are apparent in behavior. In the first months of life, infants exhibit recognition memory for all manner of natural and artificial stimuli."

Number Sense

Number sense refers to children's concepts of numbers and the relationships among number concepts. Research findings indicate that infants as young as five months of age are sensitive to number and are able to discriminate among small sets of up to three objects (Starkey and Cooper 1980; Starkey, Spelke, and Gelman 1990). Infants demonstrate the ability to quickly and accurately recognize the quantity in a small set of objects without counting. This ability is called subitizing.

According to one theoretical perspective, infants' abilities to discriminate among numbers, for example, two versus three objects, does not reflect "number knowledge." Rather, this early skill appears to be based on infants' perceptual abilities to "see" small arrangements of number (Clements 2004; Carey 2001), or on their ability to notice a change in the general amount of objects they are seeing (Mix, Huttenlocher, and Levine 2002). The alternative view is that the infant's early sensitivity to number is numerical in nature. In other words, infants have a capacity to distinguish among numbers and to reason about these numbers in numerically meaningful ways (Wynn 1998; Gallistel and Gelman 1992). In some sense, they know that three objects are more than one object. Whether early number sensitivity is solely perceptual in nature or also numerical in nature, developmental theorists agree that it sets the foundation for the later development of children's understanding of number and quantity.

As children's understanding and use of language increases, they begin to assimilate language based on number knowledge to their nonverbal knowledge of number and quantity (Baroody 2004). Between 18 and 24 months of age, children use relational words to indicate "more" or "same" as well as number words. They begin to count aloud, typically starting with "one" and continuing with a stream of number names (Fuson 1988; Gelman and Gallistel 1978), although they may omit some numbers and not use the conventional number list (e.g. "one, two, three, seven, nine, ten"). Around the same age, children also begin to count small collections of objects; however, they may point to the same item twice or say a number word without pointing to an object. And they begin to construct an understanding of cardinality (i.e., the last number word is used when counting represents the total number of objects).

Classification

Classification refers to the infant's developing ability to group, sort, categorize, connect, and have expectations of objects and people according to their attributes. Three-month-olds demonstrate that they expect people to act differently than objects (Legerstee 1997). They also demonstrate the ability to discriminate between smiling and frowning expressions (Barrera and Maurer 1981). Mandler (2000) distinguishes between two types of categorization made by infants: perceptual and conceptual. Perceptual categorization has to do with similarities or differences infants sense, such as similarities in visual appearance. Conceptual categorization has to do with grouping based on what objects do or how they act. According to Mareschal and French (2000, 59), "the ability to categorize underlies much of cognition." Classification is a fundamental skill in both problem solving and symbolic play.

Symbolic Play

Symbolic play is a common early childhood behavior also called "pretend play, make-believe play, fantasy play . . . or imaginative play" (Gowen 1995, 75). Representational thinking is a core component of symbolic play. At around eight months of age, infants have learned the functions of common objects (for example, holding a play telephone to "hear" Grandma's voice). By the time children are around 18 months of age, they use one object to stand for, or represent, another. For example, an 18-month-old may pretend a banana is a telephone. At around 36 months, children engage in make-believe play in which they represent an object without having that object, or a concrete substitute, available. For example, they may make a "phone call" by holding their hand up to their ear.

As children approach 36 months of age, they increasingly engage in pretend play in which they reenact familiar events. Make-believe play allows older infants to try to better understand social roles, engage in communication with others, and revisit and make sense of past experiences. Research suggests that engaging in pretend play appears to be related to young children's developing understanding of other people's feelings and beliefs (Youngblade and Dunn 1995). Outdoor environments, such as sandboxes (Moser 1995) or play structures, offer rich opportunities for symbolic play or pretending. Although outdoor play areas are often considered most in terms of motor behavior or physical activity, they also offer special opportunities for symbolic play (Perry 2003). For example, children playing outside may pretend to garden or may use a large wheeled toy to reenact going on a shopping trip.

Attention Maintenance

Attention maintenance has been described as a form of cognitive self-regulation. It refers to the infant's growing ability to exercise control over his attention or concentration (Bronson 2000). Attention maintenance permits infants to gather information, to sustain learning experiences, to observe, and to problem-solve. Infants demonstrate attention maintenance when they attend to people, actions, and things they find interesting even in the presence of distractions. The ability to maintain attention/concentration is an important self-regulatory skill related to learning. There is significant variability in attentiveness even among typically developing children (Ruff and Rothbart 1996).

Understanding of Personal Care Routines

Personal care activities are a routine part of the young child's daily life. They also present significant opportunities for learning in both child care settings and at home. Infants' growing abilities to anticipate, understand, and participate in these routines represent a significant aspect of their cognitive functioning, one related to their abilities to understand their relationships with others, their abilities to take care of themselves, and their skills in group participation. At first, young infants respond to the adult's actions during these routines. Then they begin to participate more actively (O'Brien 1997). Understanding the steps involved in personal care routines and anticipating next steps are skills related to the cognitive foundations of attention maintenance, imitation, memory, cause-and-effect, and problem solving. The cultural perspectives of the adults who care for infants are related to their expectations for the degree of independence or self-initiation children demonstrate during personal care routines. Depending on their cultural experiences, children may vary greatly in their understanding of personal care routines.

Foundation: Cause-and-Effect

The developing understanding that one event brings about another

8 months	18 months	36 months
At around eight months of age, children perform simple actions to make things happen, notice the relationships between events, and notice the effects of others on the immediate environment.	At around 18 months of age, children combine simple actions to cause things to happen or change the way they interact with objects and people in order to see how it changes the outcome.	At around 36 months of age, children demonstrate an understanding of cause and effect by making predictions about what could happen and reflect upon what caused something to happen. (California Department of Education [CDE] 2005)
For example, the child may:	**For example, the child may:**	**For example, the child may:**
• Shake a toy, hear the sound it makes, and then shake it again. (5.5–8 mos.; Parks 2004, 58) • Loudly bang a spoon on the table, notice the loud sound, and do it again. (By 7 mos.; American Academy of Pediatrics 2004, 210; 8 mos.; Meisels and others 2003, 21) • Watch the infant care teacher wind up a music box and, when the music stops, touch her hand to get her to make it start again. (5–9 mos.; Parks 2004, 58) • Splash hands in water and notice how his face gets wet. (4–10 mos.; Ginsburg and Opper 1988, 43) • Push a button on the push-button toy and watch the figure pop up. (6–9 mos.; Lerner and Ciervo 2003) • Put objects into a clear container, turn it over and watch the objects fall out, and then fill it up again. (8 mos.; Meisels and others 2003, 21) • Clap hands and then look at a parent to get her to play pat-a-cake. (8 mos.; Meisels and others 2003, 21)	• Try to wind the handle of a popup toy after not being able to open the top. (15 mos.; Brazelton 1992, 161) • Drop different objects from various heights to see how they fall and to hear the noise they make when they land. (12–18 mos.; Ginsburg and Opper 1988, 56) • Build a tower with the big cardboard blocks and kick it over to make it fall, then build it again and knock it down with a hand. (18 mos.; Meisels and others 2003, 37) • Use a wooden spoon to bang on different pots and pans, and notice how the infant care teacher responds when the child hits the pans harder and makes a louder noise. (18 mos.; Meisels and others 2003, 37)	• Communicate, "She misses her mommy" when a child cries after her mother leaves in the morning. • Make a prediction about what will happen next in the story when the infant care teacher asks, "What do you think will happen next?" • Answer the infant care teacher when she asks, "What do you think your mom's going to say when you give her your picture?" • See a bandage on a peer's knee and ask, "What happened?" • Push the big green button to make the tape recorder play. (By 36 mos.; American Academy of Pediatrics 2004, 308) • Walk quietly when the baby is sleeping.

Chart continues on next page.

Behaviors leading up to the foundation (4 to 7 months)	Behaviors leading up to the foundation (9 to 17 months)	Behaviors leading up to the foundation (19 to 35 months)
During this period, the child may:	During this period, the child may:	During this period, the child may:
• Hear a loud noise and turn head in the direction of the noise. (3.5–5 mos.; Parks 2004, 37)	• Hold a block in each hand and bang the blocks together. (8.5–12 mos.; Parks 2004)	• Roll cars of different sizes down the slide. (18–24 mos.; Lerner and Ciervo 2003)
• Explore toys with hands and mouth. (3–6 mos.; Parks 2004, 10)	• Keep turning an object around to find the side that makes it work, such as a reflective side of a mirror, or the open side of a nesting cup. (9–12 mos.; Parks 2004, 65)	
• Move body in a rocking motion to get the infant care teacher to continue rocking. (4–5 mos.; Parks 2004, 57; Birth–8 mos.; Lerner and Dombro 2000)	• Cry and anticipate that the infant care teacher will come to help. (9–12 mos.; Lerner and Ciervo 2003)	
• Kick legs in the crib and notice that the mobile up above jiggles with the kicking movements. (4–5 mos.; American Academy of Pediatrics 2004, 209)	• Drop an object repeatedly from the chair to hear it clang on the floor or to get the infant care teacher to come pick it up. (9–12 mos.; Parks 2004, 65)	
• Attend to a toy while exploring it with the hands. (Scaled score for 9 for 5:16–6:15 mos.; Bayley 2006, 55)	• Watch the infant care teacher squeeze the toy in the water table to make water squirt out, then try the same action. (Scaled score of 10 for 13:16–14:15 mos.; Bayley 2006, 61)	
	• Hand a toy car to a family member after it stops moving and the child cannot figure out how to make it move again. (12–15 mos.; Parks 2005, 59)	
	• Close eyes and turn face away from the water table before splashing with hands. (12 mos.; Meisels and others 2003, 28)	
	• Continue to push the button on a toy that is broken and appear confused to frustrated when nothing happens. (12 mos.; Meisels and others 2003, 29)	

Foundation: Spatial Relationships

The developing understanding of how things move and fit in space

8 months	18 months	36 months
At around eight months of age, children move their bodies, explore the size and shape of objects, and observe people and objects as they move through space.	At around 18 months of age, children use trial and error to discover how things move and fit in space. (12–18 mos.; Parks 2004, 81)	At around 36 months of age, children can predict how things will fit and move in space without having to try out every possible solution, and show understanding of words used to describe size and locations in space.
For example, the child may:	**For example, the child may:**	**For example, the child may:**
• Use vision or hearing to track the path of someone walking by. (5.5–8 mos.; Parks 2004, 64; birth–8 mos.; Lally and others 1995, 78–79) • Watch a ball roll away after accidentally knocking it. (5.5–8 mos., Parks 2004, 64) • Hold one stacking cup in each hand. (6.5–7.5 mos.; Parks 2004, 50) • Put toys into a clear container, dump them out, and then fill the container up again. (8 mos.; Meisels and others 2003, 21)	• Go around the back of a chair to get the toy car that rolled behind it instead of trying to follow the car's path by squeezing underneath the chair. (12–18 mos.; Parks 2004 67; 8–18 mos.; Lally and others 1995, 78–79) • Use two hands to pick up a big truck, but only one hand to pick up a small one. (12–18 mos.; Parks 2004, 81) • Put a smaller nesting cup inside a larger cup after trying it the other way around. (12–18 mos.; Parks 2004, 81) • Choose a large cookie off the plate instead of a smaller one. (12–18 mos.; Parks 2004, 81) • Put the child-sized hat on his head and the larger hat on the infant care teacher's head. (12–18 mos.; Parks 2004, 81) • Stack three nesting cups inside one another, after trying some combinations that do not work. (12–19 mos.; Parks 2004, 82) • Put one or two pegs into the peg-board. (14:16–15:15 mos.; Bayley 2006, 62) • Roll a ball back and forth with the infant care teacher. (18 mos.; Meisels and others 2003, 38) • Fit pieces into a puzzle board. (18 mos.; Meisels and others 2003, 39) • Try to fit a piece into the shape sorter and, when it does not fit, turn it until it fits. (12–19 mos.; Parks 2004, 82)	• Hand the big truck to a peer who asks for the big one. (Scaled score of 10 for 28:16–30:15 mos.; Bayley 2006, 95) • Use words such as big and little. (25–30 mos.; Parks 2004, 82; 36 mos.; Meisels and others 2003, 73) • Put together a puzzle with three to four separate pieces. (By 36 mos.; American Academy of Pediatrics 2004, 308; 30–36 mos.; Parks 2004, 68) • Get the serving spoon off the tray when the infant care teacher asks for the big spoon, even though there are small spoons on the tray. (30–36 mos.; Parks 2004, 83) • Stack rings onto a post with the biggest ring on the bottom and the smallest ring on the top, without much trial and error. (30–36 mos.; Parks 2004, 83; 24–36 mos.; *Engaging Young Children* 2004, 44) • Point to a peer's stick when the infant care teacher asks which stick is longer. (33–36 mos.; Parks 2004, 83; 24–36 mos.; *Engaging Young Children* 2004, 53) • Understand requests that include simple prepositions; for example, "Please put your cup on the table" or "Please get your blanket out of your back pack." (By 36 mos.; Coplan 1993, 2; by 36 mos.; American Academy of Pediatrics 2004; 24–36 mos.; *Engaging Young Children* 2004) • Move around an obstacle when going from one place to another. (24–36 mos.; American Academy of Pediatrics 2004, 303)

Chart continues on next page.

Behaviors leading up to the foundation (4 to 7 months)	Behaviors leading up to the foundation (9 to 17 months)	Behaviors leading up to the foundation (19 to 35 months)
During this period, the child may:	During this period, the child may:	During this period, the child may:
• Look at her own hand. (Scaled score of 9 for 4:06–4:15 mos.; Bayley 2006, 53)	• Roll a car back and forth on the floor. (6–11 mos.; Parks 2004, 26)	• Complete a puzzle of three separate cut-out pieces, such as a circle, square, and triangle. (Scaled score of 10 for 19:16–20:15 mos.; Bayley 2006, 66)
• Reach for a nearby toy and try to grasp it. (4.5–5.5 mos.; Parks 2004; scaled score of 10 for 4:16–4:25 mos.; Bayley 2006, 54)	• Dump toys out of a container. (9–11 mos.; Parks 2004, 64)	• Fit many pegs into a pegboard. (Scaled score of 10 for 21:16–22:15 mos.; Bayley 2006, 68)
• Explore toys with hands and mouth. (3–6 mos.; Parks 2004, 10)	• Turn a toy to explore all sides to figure out how it works. (9–12 mos.; Parks 2004, 65)	• Turn a book right-side up after realizing that it is upside down. (18–24 mos.; Parks 2004)
	• Throw or drop a spoon or cup from the table and watch as it falls. (9–12 mos.; Parks 2004, 65)	• Fit four nesting cups in the correct order, even if it takes a couple of tries. (19–24 mos.; Parks 2004, 82)
	• Take rings off a stacking ring toy. (10–11 mos.; Parks 2004, 65)	• Assemble a two-piece puzzle; for example, a picture of a flower cut into two pieces. (Scaled score of 10 for 23:16–24:15 mos.; Bayley 2006, 69)
	• Move over and between cushions and pillows on the floor. (8–12 mos.; American Academy of Pediatrics 2004, 234)	
	• Crawl down a few carpeted stairs. (Around 12 mos.; American Academy of Pediatrics 2004, 234)	
	• See a ball roll under the couch and then reach under the couch. (12–13 mos.; Parks 2004, 66)	
	• Stack one block on top of another one. (12–16 mos.; Parks 2004, 66)	
	• Put one or two rings back onto the post of a stacking ring toy. (13–15 mos.; Parks 2004, 66)	
	• Put the circle piece of a puzzle into the round opening, after trying the triangle opening and the square opening. (Scaled score of 10 for 15:16–16:15 mos.; Bayley 2006, 63)	

Foundation: Problem Solving

The developing ability to engage in a purposeful effort to reach a goal or figure out how something works

8 months	18 months	36 months
At around eight months of age, children use simple actions to try to solve problems involving objects, their bodies, or other people.	At around 18 months of age, children use a number of ways to solve problems: physically trying out possible solutions before finding one that works; using objects as tools; watching someone else solve the problem and then applying the same solution; or gesturing or vocalizing to someone else for help	At around 36 months of age, children solve some problems without having to physically try out every possible solution and may ask for help when needed. (By 36 mos.; American Academy of Pediatrics 2004, 308)
For example, the child may:	**For example, the child may:**	**For example, the child may:**
• Shake, bang, and squeeze toys repeatedly to make the sounds happen again and again. (5.5–8 mos.; Parks 2004, 58; by 12 mos.; American Academy of Pediatrics 2004, 243) • Reach for a ball as it rolls away. (5.5–8 mos.; Parks 2004, 64) • Vocalize to get the infant care teacher's attention. (6.5–8 mos.; Parks 2004) • Pull the string on a toy to make it come closer. (8 mos.; Meisels and others 2003, 21) • Focus on a desired toy that is just out of reach while repeatedly reaching for it. (5–9 mos.; Parks 2004, 49) • Turn the bottle over to get the nipple in his mouth. • Lift up a scarf to search for a toy that is hidden underneath. (By 8 mos.; American Academy of Pediatrics 2004, 244)	• Pull the string of a pull toy to get it closer even when the toy gets momentarily stuck on something. (18 mos.; Meisels and others 2003, 38) • Use the handle of a toy broom to dislodge a ball under the bookshelf. (8–18 mos.; Lally and others 1995, 78–79) • Bring a small stool over to reach a toy on top of a shelf, having observed the infant care teacher do it. (8–18 mos.; Lally and others 1995, 78–79) • Look at a plate of crackers that is out of reach and then at the infant care teacher, and communicate "more." (Scaled score of 10 for 16:16–17:15 mos.; Bayley 2006; 14–20 mos.; Parks 2004) • Hand the infant care teacher a puzzle piece that the child is having trouble with.	• Ignore the stick that is much too short to reach a desired object and choose a stick that looks as if it may be long enough. • Stack only the cubes with holes in them on the stacking post, ignoring the cube-shaped blocks without holes that got mixed into the bin. (18–36 mos.; Lally and others 1995, 78–79) • Place the triangle piece into the puzzle without first needing to try it in the round or square hole. (By 36 mos.; American Academy of Pediatrics 2004, 306) • Ask the infant care teacher for help with the lid of a jar of paint. (36 mos.; Meisels and others 2003, 75) • Ask a peer to help move the train tracks over so that the child can build a block tower on the floor. (36 mos.; Meisels and others 2003, 75) • Ask or gesture for the infant care teacher to help tie the child's shoelace. (36 mos.; Meisels and others 2003, 75)

Chart continues on next page.

Behaviors leading up to the foundation (4 to 7 months)	Behaviors leading up to the foundation (9 to 17 months)	Behaviors leading up to the foundation (19 to 35 months)
During this period, the child may: • Explore toys with hands and mouth. (3–6 mos.; Parks 2004, 10) • Reach for a second toy when already holding on to one toy. (5–6.5 mos.; Parks 2004, 49) • Hold a toy up to look at it while exploring it with the hands. (Scaled score of 9 for 5:16–6:15 mos.; Bayley 2006, 55)	During this period, the child may: • Crawl over a pile of soft blocks to get to the big red ball. (8–11 mos.; Parks 2004) • Figure out how toys work by repeating the same actions over and over again. (9–12 mos.; Lerner and Ciervo 2003) • Pull the blanket in order to obtain the toy that is lying out of reach on top of the blanket. (8–10 mos.; Parks 2004) • Crawl around the legs of a chair to get to the ball that rolled behind it. (9–12 mos.; Parks 2004, 50; 18 mos.; Lally and others 1995, 78–79) • Keep turning an object around to find the side that makes it work, such as the reflective side of a mirror or the open side of a nesting cup. (9–12 mos.; Parks 2004, 65) • Try to hold on to two toys with one hand while reaching for a third desired toy, even if not successful. (Scaled score of 9 for 10:16–11:15 mos.; Bayley 2006, 58) • Unscrew the lid of a plastic jar to get items out of it. (Scaled score of 10 for 14:16–15:15 mos.; Bayley 2006, 62)	During this period, the child may: • Use a stick to dig in the sandbox when unable to find a shovel. (17–24 mos.; Parks 2004) • Use a tool to solve a problem, such as using the toy broom to get a car out from under the couch, using a wooden puzzle base as a tray to carry all the puzzle pieces to another place, or using the toy shopping cart to pick up the wooden blocks and move them to the shelf to be put away. (17–24 mos.; Parks 2004, 52) • Move to the door and try to turn the knob after a parent leaves for work in the morning. (21–23 mos.; Parks 2004, 53) • Imitate a problem-solving method that the child has observed someone else do before. (Scaled score of 10 for 20:16–21:15 mos.; Bayley 2006, 66) • Tug on shoelaces in order to untie them. • Complete a puzzle with three separate cut-out pieces, such as a circle, square, and triangle, even though the child may try to put the triangle into the square hole before fitting it in the triangle opening. (Scaled score of 10 for 19:16–20:15 mos.; Bayley 2006, 66)

Foundation: Imitation

The developing ability to mirror, repeat, and practice the actions of others, either immediately or later

8 months	18 months	36 months
At around 8 months of age, children imitate simple actions and expressions of others during interactions	At around 18 months of age, children imitate others' actions that have more than one step and imitate simple actions that they have observed others doing at an earlier time. (Parks 2004; 28)	At around 36 months of age, children reenact multiple steps of others' actions that they have observed at an earlier time. (30–36 mos.; Parks 2004, 29)
For example, the child may:	**For example, the child may:**	**For example, the child may:**
• Copy the infant care teacher's movements when playing pat-a-cake and peek-a-boo. (Coplan 1993, 3) • Imitate a familiar gesture, such as clapping hands together or patting a doll's back, after seeing the infant care teacher do it. (7–8 mos.; Parks 2004) • Notice how the infant care teacher makes a toy work and then push the same button to make it happen again. (6–9 mos.; Lerner and Ciervo 2003)	• Imitate simple actions that she has observed adults doing; for example, take a toy phone out of a purse and say hello as a parent does. (12–18 mos.; Lerner and Ciervo 2003) • Pretend to sweep with a child sized broom, just as a family member does at home. (15–18 mos.; Parks 2004, 27) • Rock the baby doll to sleep, just as a parent does with the new baby. (15–18 mos.; Parks 2004, 27) • Imitate using the toy hammer as a parent did. (18 mos.; Meisels and others 2003, 38)	• Reenact the steps of a family celebration that the child attended last weekend. (29–36 mos.; Hart and Risley 1999, 118–19) • Pretend to get ready for work or school by making breakfast, packing lunch, grabbing a purse, and communicating good-bye before heading out the door. (30–36 mos.; Parks 2004, 29)

Chart continues on next page.

Imitation

Behaviors leading up to the foundation (4 to 7 months)	Behaviors leading up to the foundation (9 to 17 months)	Behaviors leading up to the foundation (19 to 35 months)
During this period, the child may: • Listen to the infant care teacher talk during a diaper change and then babble back when she pauses. (5.5–6.5 mos.; Parks 2004, 125) • Copy the intonation of the infant care teacher's speech when babbling. (7 mos.; Parks 2004)	During this period, the child may: • Shrug shoulders after the infant care teacher does it. (9–11 mos.; Parks 2004; by 12 mos.; American Academy of Pediatrics 2004, 243) • Imitate sounds or words immediately after the infant care teacher makes them. (9 mos.; Apfel and Provence 2001; 12–18 mos.; Hulit and Howard 2006, 122; 17 mos.; Hart and Risley 1999, 84) • Copy the infant care teacher in waving "bye-bye" to a parent as he leaves the room. (12 mos.; Meisels and others 2003, 26) • Copy an adult's action that is unfamiliar but that the child can see herself do, such as wiggling toes, even though it may take some practice before doing it exactly as the adult does. (9–14 mos.; Parks 2004, 32) • Watch the infant care teacher squeeze the toy in the water table to make water squirt out, then try the same action. (Scaled score of 10 for 13:16–14:15 mos.; Bayley 2006, 61) • Imitate the hand motion of the infant care teacher. (Scaled score of 10 for 14:16–15:15 mos.; Bayley 2006, 135) • Point to or indicate an object, pay attention as the infant care teacher labels the object, and then try to repeat the label. (11–16 mos.; Hart and Risley 1999, 82)	During this period, the child may: • Repeat the most important word of a sentence the infant care teacher has just communicated. (17–19 mos.; Parks 2004) • Imitate the last word or last few words of what an adult just said; for example say, cup or a cup after the infant care teacher says, "That's a cup" or say, "Daddy bye-bye" after the mother says, "Daddy went bye-bye." (22 mos.; Hart and Risley 1999, 99; 17–19 mos.; Parks 2004, 128) • Copy several actions that the child cannot see himself doing, such as wrinkling the nose. (17–20 mos.; Parks 2004, 32) • Say, "beep, beep, beep, beep" after hearing the garbage truck back up outside. (18-21 mos.; Parks 2004) • Act out a few steps of a familiar routine, such as pretend to fill the tub, bathe a baby doll, and dry the doll. (18–24 mos.; Parks 2004, 28) • Imitate words that the adult has expressed to the child at an earlier time, not immediately after hearing them. (24–27 mos.; Parks 2004; 19–28 mos.; Hart and Risley 1999, 61) • Imitate two new actions of the infant care teacher; for example, put one hand on head and point with the other hand. (26:16–27:15 mos.; Bayley 2006, 71) • Imitate the way a family member communicates by using the same gestures, unique words, and intonation.

Foundation: Memory

The developing ability to store and later retrieve information about past experiences

8 months	*18 months*	*36 months*
At around 8 months of age, children recognize familiar people, objects, and routines in the environment and show awareness that familiar people still exist even when they are no longer physically present.	At around 18 months of age, children remember typical actions of people, the location of objects, and steps of routines.	At around 36 months of age, children anticipate the series of steps in familiar activities, events, or routines; remember characteristics of the environment or people in it; and may briefly describe recent past events or act them out. (24–36 mos.; Seigel 1999, 33)
For example, the child may:	**For example, the child may:**	**For example, the child may:**
• Turn toward the front door when hearing the doorbell ring or toward the phone when hearing the phone ring. (8 mos.; Meisels and others 2003, 20) • Look for the father after he briefly steps out of the child care room during drop-off in the morning. (8 mos.; Meisels and others 2003, 20)	• Get a blanket from the doll cradle because that is where baby blankets are usually stored, after the infant care teacher says, "The baby is tired. Where's her blanket?" (15–18 mos.; Parks 2004, 67) • Anticipate and participate in the steps of a nap routine. (18 mos.; Fogel 2001, 368) • Watch the infant care teacher placing a toy inside one of three pots with lids and reach for the correct lid when the teacher asks where the toy went. (8–18 mos.; Lally and others 1995, 78–79) • Continue to search for an object even though it is hidden under something distracting, such as a soft blanket or a crinkly piece of paper. • See a photo of a close family member and say his name or hug the photo. • Go to the cubby to get his blanket that is inside the diaper bag.	• Communicate, "Big slide" after a trip to neighborhood park. (24–36 mos.; Seigel 1999, 33) • Tell a parent, "Today we jumped in the puddles" when picked up from school. (Siegel 1999, 34) • Recall an event in the past, such as the time a family member came to school and made a snack. (18–36 mos.; Siegel 1999, 46) • Identify which child is absent from school that day by looking around the snack table and figuring out who is missing. (18–36 mos.; Lally and others 1995, 78–79) • Act out a trip to the grocery store by getting a cart, putting food in it, and paying for the food. (24 mos.; Bauer and Mandler 1989) • Get her pillow out of the cubby, in anticipation of naptime as soon as lunch is finished.

Chart continues on next page.

Memory

Behaviors leading up to the foundation (4 to 7 months)	Behaviors leading up to the foundation (9 to 17 months)	Behaviors leading up to the foundation (19 to 35 months)
During this period, the child may: • Explore toys with hands and mouth. (3–6 mos.; Parks 2004, 10) • Find a rattle hidden under a blanket when only the handle is showing. (4–6 mos.; Parks 2004, 42) • Look toward the floor when the bottle falls off table. (Scaled score of 10 for 5:06–5:15 mos.; Bayley 2006, 55; 8 mos.; Meisels and others 2003, 20; birth–8 mos.; Lally and others 1995, 72)	During this period, the child may: • Ask for a parent after morning drop-off. (9–12 mos.; Lerner and Ciervo 2003) • Reach in the infant care teacher's pocket after watching him hide a toy there. (11–13 mos.; Parks 2004, 43) • Look or reach inside a container of small toys after seeing the infant care teacher take the toys off the table and put them in the container. (Scaled score of 10 for 8:16–9:15 mos.; Bayley 2006, 57; birth–8 mos.; Lally and others 1995, 78–79) • Lift a scarf to search for a toy after seeing the infant care teacher hide it under the scarf. (By 8 mos.; American Academy of Pediatrics 2004, 244; 8 mos.; Kail 1990, 112)	During this period, the child may: • Say "meow" when the infant care teacher points to the picture of the cat and asks what the cat says. (12–24 mos.; Siegel 1999, 32) • Give another child an object that belongs to her. (12–24 mos.; Siegel 1999, 32) • Remember where toys should be put away in the classroom. (21–24 mos.; Parks 2004, 318) • Find a hidden toy, even when it is hidden under two or three blankets. (By 24 mos.; American Academy of Pediatrics 2004, 273) • Express "mama" when the infant care teacher asks who packed the child's snack.

Foundation: Number Sense
The developing understanding of number and quantity

8 months	18 months	36 months
At around eight months of age, children usually focus on one object or person at a time, yet they may at times hold two objects, one in each hand.	At around 18 months of age, children demonstrate understanding that there are different amounts of things.	At around 36 months of age, children show some understanding that numbers represent how many and demonstrate understanding of words that identify how much. (By 36 mos.; American Academy of Pediatrics 2004, 308)
For example, the child may:	**For example, the child may:**	**For example, the child may:**
• Hold one block in each hand, then drop one of them when the infant care teacher holds out a third block for the child to hold. (6.5–7.5 mos.; Parks 2004, 50) • Watch a ball as it rolls away after hitting it with her hand. (5.5–8 mos.; Parks 2004, 64) • Explore one toy at a time by shaking, banging, or squeezing it. (5.5–8 mos.; Parks 2004, 58; 8 mos.; Meisels and others 2003, 21; birth–8 mos.; Lally and others 1995, 78–79) • Notice when someone walks in the room.	• Communicate "more" and point to a bowl of apple slices. (18 mos.; Meisels and others 2003, 37) • Shake head "no" when offered more pasta. (18 mos.; Meisels and others 2003, 37) • Make a big pile of trucks and a little pile of trucks. • Use hand motions or words to indicate "All gone" when finished eating. (12–19 mos.; Parks 2004, 122) • Put three cars in a row.	• Pick out one object from a box or point to the picture with only one of something. (Scaled score of 10 for 35:16–36:15 mos.; Bayley 2006, 97; 24–30 mos.; Parks 2004) • Reach into bowl and take out two pieces of pear when the infant care teacher says, "Just take two." (30–36 mos.; Parks 2004) • Start counting with one, sometimes pointing to the same item twice when counting, or using numbers out of order; for example, "one, two, three, five, eight." (36 mos.; *Engaging Young Children* 2004, 178) • Use fingers to count a small number of items. (around 36 mos.; Coplan 1993, 3) • Look at a plate and quickly respond "two," without having to count, when the infant care teacher asks how many pieces of cheese there are. (36 mos.; *Engaging Young Children* 2004, 178) • Hold up two fingers when asked, "Show me two" or "How old are you?" (36 mos.; *Engaging Young Children* 2004, 178; by 36 mos.; American Academy of Pediatrics 2004, 308) • Identify "more" with collections of up to four items, without needing to count them. (36 mos.; *Engaging Young Children* 2004, 31 and 180) • Use more specific words to communicate how many, such as a little or a lot. (Hulit and Howard 2006, 186)

Chart continues on next page.

Number Sense

Behaviors leading up to the foundation (4 to 7 months)	Behaviors leading up to the foundation (9 to 17 months)	Behaviors leading up to the foundation (19 to 35 months)
During this period, the child may: • Explore toys with hands and mouth. (3–6 mos.; Parks 2004, 10) • Reach for second toy but may not grasp it when already holding one toy in the other hand. (5–6.5 mos.; Parks 2004, 49; scaled score of 10 for 5:16–6:15 mos.; Bayley 2006, 55) • Transfer a toy from one hand to the other. (5.5–7 mos.; Parks 2004) • Reach for, grasp, and hold onto a toy with one hand when already holding a different toy in the other hand. (Scaled score of 10 for 6:16–7:15 mos.; Bayley 2006, 56) • Track visually the path of a moving object. (6–8 mos.; Parks 2004, 64)	During this period, the child may: • Try to hold onto two toys with one hand while reaching for a third desired toy, even if not successful. (Scaled score of 9 for 10:16–11:15 mos.; Bayley 2006, 58; 8–10 mos.; Parks 2004, 50) • Hold a block in each hand and bang them together. (8.5–12 mos.; Parks 2004) • Put several pegs into a plastic container and then dump them into a pile. (12–13 mos.; Parks 2004, 65)	During this period, the child may: • Get two cups from the cupboard when playing in the housekeeping area with a friend. (21 mos.; Mix, Huttenlocher, and Levine 2002) • Look at or point to the child with one piece of apple left on his napkin when the infant care teacher asks, "Who has just one piece of apple?" (24–30 mos.; Parks 2004, 74) • Give the infant care teacher one cracker from a pile of many when she asks for "one." (25–30 mos.; Parks 2004; scaled score of 10 for 28:16–30:15 mos.; Bayley 2006, 73)

Foundation: Classification

The developing ability to group, sort, categorize, connect, and have expectations of objects and people according to their attributes

8 months	*18 months*	*36 months*
At around eight months of age, children distinguish between familiar and unfamiliar people, places, and objects and explore the differences between them. (Barrera and Mauer 1981)	At around 18 months of age, children show awareness when objects are in some way connected to each other, match two objects that are the same, and separate a pile of objects into two groups based on one attribute. (Mandler and McDonough 1998)	At around 36 months of age, children group objects into multiple piles based on one attribute at a time, put things that are similar but not identical into one group, and may label each grouping, even though sometimes these labels are overgeneralized. (36 mos.; Mandler and McDonough 1993)
For example, the child may:	**For example, the child may:**	**For example, the child may:**
<ul><li>Explore how one toy feels and then explore how another toy feels.</li><li>Stare at an unfamiliar person and move toward a familiar person.</li></ul>	<ul><li>Look at the crayons before choosing color. (12-18 mos.; Parks 2004, 77)</li><li>Choose usually to play with the blue ball even though there I a red one just like it. (12–18 mos.; Parks 2004, 77)</li><li>Pick the toy car from the bin filled with toy dishes. (15–18 mos.; Parks 2004, 77)</li><li>Pack the baby doll's blanket, brush, bottle, and clothes into a backpack. (15–19 mos.; Parks 2004, 77)</li><li>Match two identical toys; for example, find another fire truck when the infant care teacher asks, "Can you find a truck just like that one?" (15-19 mos.; Parks 2004, 77)</li><li>Place all toy cars on one side of the rug and all blocks on the other side. (15–18 mos.; Parks 2004, 77)</li></ul>	<ul><li>Identify a few colors when they are named; for example, get a red ball from the bin of multicolored balls when the infant care teacher asks for the red one. (Scaled score of 10 for 34:16–36 mos.; Bayley 2006, 97; 33 mos.+; Parks 2004, 79)</li><li>Make three piles of tangrams in various shapes, such as a circle, square and triangle. (30–36 mos.; Parks 2004, 79)</li><li>Pick two big pears from a bowl containing two big pears and two small pears, even if the big pears are different colors. (Scaled score of 10 for 30:16–33;15 mos.; Bayley 2004, 74)</li><li>Sort primary-colored blocks into three piles; a red pile, a yellow pile, and a blue one. (33 mos.+; Parks 2004, 79; 32 mos.; Bayley 2006.)</li><li>Point to different pictures of houses in a book even though all of the houses look different. (30–36 mos.; Parks 2004, 79)</li><li>Put all the soft stuffed animals in one pile and all the hard plastic toy animals in another pile and label the piles "soft animals: and "hard animals." (18–36 mos.; Lally and others 1995, 78-79)</li><li>Call all four-legged animals at the farm "cows," even though some are actually sheep and others horses. (18-36 mos.; Lally and others 1995, 78-79)</li></ul>

Chart continues on next page.

Classification

Behaviors leading up to the foundation (4 to 7 months)	Behaviors leading up to the foundation (9 to 17 months)	Behaviors leading up to the foundation (19 to 35 months)
During this period, the child may: • Explore toys with hands and mouth. (3–6 mos.; Parks 2004, 10) • Bang a toy on the table. (5.5–7 mos.; Parks 2004, 25) • Touch different objects (e.g., hard or soft) differently.	During this period, the child may: • Roll a car back and forth on the floor, then roll a ball. (6–11 mos.; Parks 2004, 26) • Use two items that go together; for example, brush a doll's hair with a brush, put a spoon in a bowl, or use a hammer to pound an object. (9–15 mos.; Parks 2004, 26–27; by 12 mos.; American Academy of Pediatrics 2004, 243) • Put the red blocks together when the infant care teacher asks, "Which blocks go together?"	During this period, the child may: • Point to or indicate the realistic-looking plastic cow when the infant care teacher holds up a few toy animals and says, "Who says 'moo'?" (18–22 mos.; Parks 2004, 85) • Sort three different kinds of toys; for example, put the puzzle pieces in the puzzle box, the blocks in the block bin, and the toy animals in the basket during clean-up time. (19–24 mos.; Parks 2004, 77) • Show understanding of what familiar objects are supposed to be used for, such as knowing that a hat is for wearing or a tricycle is for riding. (Scaled score of 10 for 23:16–25 mos.; Bayley 2006, 93) • Pick a matching card from a pile of cards. (Scaled score of 10 for 24:16–25 mos.; Bayley 2006, 70) • Point to or indicate all the green cups at the lunch table. (26 mos.; Bayley 2006) • Call the big animals "mama" and the small animals "baby." (27 mos.; Bayley 2006) • Help the infant care teacher sort laundry into two piles; whites and colors. (28 mos.; Hart and Risley 1999, 95) • Put the red marker back in the red can, the blue marker back in the blue can, and the yellow marker back in the yellow can when finished coloring. (Scaled score of 10 for 26:16–28:15 mos.; Bayley 2006, 71) • Match one shape to another shape. (26-29 mos.; Parks 2004, 78; 26–29 mos.; Parks 2004)

Foundation: Symbolic Play

The developing ability to use actions, objects, or ideas to represent other actions, objects, or ideas

8 months	18 months	36 months
At around 8 months of age, children become familiar with objects and actions through active exploration. Children also build knowledge of people, action, objects and ideas through observation. (Fenson and others 1976; Rogoff and others 2003)	At around 18 months of age, children use one object to represent another object and engage in one or two simple actions of pretend play.	At around 36 months of age, children engage in make-believe play involving several sequenced steps, assigned roles, and an overall plan and sometimes pretend by imagining an object without needing the concrete object present. (30–36 mos.; Parks 2004, 29)
For example, the child may:	**For example, the child may:**	**For example, the child may:**
• Cause toys to make noise by shaking, banging and squeezing them. (5.5–8 mos.; Parks 2004, 58; by 12 mos.; American Academy of Pediatrics 2004, 243) • Roll car back and forth on floor. (6–11 mos.; Parks 2004, 26)	• Pretend to drink from an empty cup by making slurping noises and saying "ah" when finished. (Segal 2004, 39) • Begin to engage in pretend play by using a play spoon to stir in the kitchen area. (12–18 mos.; Lerner and Ciervo 2003) • Pretend that the banana is a telephone by picking it up, holding it to the ear, and saying, "Hi!" (12–18 mos.; Lerner and Ciervo 2003) • Laugh at an older brother when he puts a bowl on his head like a hat. (12–18 mos.; Parks 2004, 317 • Imitate a few steps of adult behavior during play; for example, pretend to feed the baby doll with the toy spoon and bowl. (15–18 mos.; Parks 2004, 27) • Use a rectangular wooden block as a phone. (18–24 mos.; Parks 2004, 28)	• Assign roles to self and others when playing in the dramatic play area (for example, "I'll be the daddy, you be the baby"), even though the child may not stay in her role throughout the play sequence. (30–36 mos.; Parks 2004, 29; 24 mos.; Segal 2004, 43) • Line up a row of chairs and communicate "All aboard! The train is leaving." (36 mos.; Vygotsky 1978, 111) • Use two markers to represent people in the dollhouse by moving them around as if they are walking. (36 mos.; Vygotsky 1978, 111) • Stir "cake batter" while holding an imaginary spoon or serve an invisible burrito on a plate. (30–36 mos.; Parks 2004, 29; Scaled score of 10 for 27:16–29:15 mos.; Bayley 2006, 69) • Communicate with self during pretend play to describe actions to self; for example, "Now I stir the soup." (Hart and Risley 1999, 125) • Plan with other children what they are going to pretend before starting to play; for example, "Let's play doggies!" (Segal 2004, 39; 36 mos.; Meisels and others 2003, 74) • Pretend to be a baby during dramatic play because there is a new baby at home. (36 mos.; Meisels and others 2003, 73) • Build a small town with blocks and then use the toy fire truck to pretend to put out a fire in the town. (By 36 mos.; American Academy of Pediatrics 2004, 309)

Chart continues on next page.

Behaviors leading up to the foundation (4 to 7 months)	Behaviors leading up to the foundation (9 to 17 months)	Behaviors leading up to the foundation (19 to 35 months)
During this period, the child may: • Explore toys with friends and mouth. (3–6 mos.; Parks 2004, 10)	During this period, the child may: • Use two items that go together; for example, brush a doll's hair with brush, put a spoon in a bowl, or use a hammer to pound an object through a hole. (9–15 mos.; Parks 2004, 26-27) • Use objects in pretend play the way they were intended to be used; for example, pretend to drink coffee or tea from play coffee cup. (Scaled score of 10 for 15:16–16:15 mos.; Bayley 2006, 62)	During this period, the child may: • Use the stuffed animals to play "veterinarian" one day and then to play "farmer" the next day. (18–24 mos.; Lerner and Ciervo 2003) • Communicate "Time for night-night" to a doll while playing house. (22–24 mos.; Parks 2004, 133) • Complete three or more actions in a sequence of pretend play so the actions have a beginning, middle and end, such as giving the baby doll a bath, putting his pajamas on, and putting him to sleep. (24–30 mos.; Parks 2004, 28; by 36 mos.; American Academy of Pediatrics 2004, 309; scaled score for 10 for 29:16–30:15 mos.; Bayley 2006, 73) • Pretend that the doll or stuffed animal has feelings, such as making a whining noise to indicate that the stuffed puppy is sad. (24–30 mos.; Parks 2004, 28) • Make the stuffed animals move, as if they were alive, during pretend play. (24–30 mos.; Parks 2004, 28) • Engage in extended pretend play that has a theme, such as birthday party or doctor. (24–30 mos.; Parks 2004, 29) • Use abstract things to represent other things in pretend play; for example, use dough or sand to represent a birthday cake and sticks or straws to represent candles. (24–30 mos.; Parks 2004, 29; scaled score of 10 for 24:16–25:15 mos.; Bayley 2006, 70; Segal 2004, 39)

Foundation: Attention Maintenance

The developing ability to attend to people and things while interacting with others and exploring the environment and play materials

8 months	18 months	36 months
At around eight months of age, children pay attention to different things and people in the environment in specific, distinct ways. (Bronson 2000, 64)	At around 18 months of age, children rely on order and predictability in the environment to help organize their thoughts and focus attention. (Bronson 2000, 191)	At around 36 months of age, children sometimes demonstrate the ability to pay attention to more than one thing at a time.
For example, the child may:	**For example, the child may:**	**For example, the child may:**
• Play with one toy for a few minutes before focusing on a different toy. (6–9 mos.; Parks 2004, 12 and 26; 8 mos.; American Academy of Pediatrics 2004, 241) • Focus on a desired toy that is just out of reach while repeatedly reaching for it. (5–9 mos.; Parks 2004, 49) • Show momentary attention to board books with bright colors and simple shapes. • Attend to the play of other children. • Put toy animals into a clear container, dump them out, and then fill the container up again. (8 mos.; Meisels and others 2003, 21) • Stop moving, to focus on the infant care teacher when she starts to interact with the child.	• Expect favorite songs to be sung the same way each time and protest if the infant care teacher changes the words. • Insist on following the same bedtime routine every night. • Nod and take the infant care teacher's hand when the teacher says, "I know you are sad because Shanti is using the book right now, and you would like a turn. Shall we go to the book basket and find another one to read together?"	• Realize, during clean-up time, that he has put a car in the block bin and return to put it in the proper place. • Search for and find a favorite book and ask the infant care teacher to read it. • Pound the play dough with a hammer while talking with a peer.
Behaviors leading up to the foundation (4 to 7 months)	**Behaviors leading up to the foundation (9 to 17 months)**	**Behaviors leading up to the foundation (19 to 35 months)**
During this period, the child may: • Remain calm and focused on people, interesting toys, or interesting sounds for a minute or so. (1–6 mos.; Parks 2004, 9) • Explore a toy by banging, mouthing, or looking at it. (Scaled score of 9 for 3:26–4:05 mos.; Bayley 2006, 52)	During this period, the child may: • Pay attention to the infant care teacher's voice without being distracted by other noises in the room. (9–11 mos.; Parks 2004; 12) • Focus on one toy or activity for a while when really interested. (By 12 mos.; American Academy of Pediatrics 2004, 241)	During this period, the child may: • Play alone with toys for several minutes at a time before moving on to different activity. (18–24 mos.; Parks 2004, 15) • Sit in a parent's lap to read a book together. (Scaled score of 10 for 21:16–22:15 mos.; Bayley 2006)

Foundation: Understanding of Personal Care Routines

The developing ability to understand and participate in personal care routines

8 months	18 months	36 months
At around eight months of age, children are responsive during the steps of personal care routines. (CDE 2005)	At around 18 months of age, children show awareness of familiar personal care routines and participate in the steps of those routines. (CDE 2005)	At around 36 months of age, children initiate and follow through with some personal care routines. (CDE 2005)
For example, the child may:	**For example, the child may:**	**For example, the child may:**
• Turn head away as the infant care teacher reaches with a tissue to wipe the child's nose. (8 mos.; Meisels and others 2003, 20) • Kick legs in anticipation of a diaper change and then quite down as the parent wipes the child's bottom. (CDE 2005) • Pay attention to her hands as the infant care teacher holds them under running water and helps rub them together with soap. (CDE 2005)	• Go to the sink when the infant care teacher says that it is time to wash hands. (Scaled score of 10 for 17:16–18:15 mos.; Bayley 2006, 90; 12–18 mos.; Lerner and Ciervo 2003; 12 mos.; Coplan 1993, 2; by 24 mos.; American Academy of Pediatrics 2004; 24 mos.; Meisels and others 2003, 46) • Gets a tissue when the infant care teacher says, "Please go get a tissue. We need to wipe your nose." (18 mos.; Meisels and others 2003, 36) • Move toward the door to the playground after seeing the infant care teacher put his coat on. (18 mos.; Meisels and others 2003, 38) • Put snack dishes in the sink and the bib in the hamper after eating. • Have trouble settling down for a nap until the infant care teacher needs a story, because that is the naptime routine. (12–18 mos.; Parks 2004, 317)	• Go to the sink and wash hands after seeing snacks being set out on the table. (CDE 2005) • Get a tissue to wipe own nose or bring the tissue to the infant care teacher for help when the child feels that his nose needs to be wiped. (CDE 2005) • Take a wet shirt off when needing to put on a dry one. (36 mos.; Meisels and others 2003, 76) • Help set the table for lunchtime (36 mos.; Meisels and others 2003, 77)
Behaviors leading up to the foundation (4 to 7 months)	**Behaviors leading up to the foundation (9 to 17 months)**	**Behaviors leading up to the foundation (19 to 35 months)**
During this period, the child may: • Anticipate being fed upon seeing the infant care teacher approach with a bottle. • Hold onto the bottle while being fed by the infant care teacher. (4 mos.; Meisels and others 2003, 14)	During this period, the child may: • Cooperate during a diaper change by lifting her bottom. (10.5–12 mos.; Parks 2004) • Grab the spoon as the infant care teacher tries to feed the child. (12 mos.; Meisels and others 2003, 31) • Raise arms when the infant care teacher tries to put a dry shirt on the child. (12 mos.; Meisels and others 2003)	During this period, the child may: • Drink from a cup without spilling much. (24 mos.; Meisels and others 2003, 52) • Try to put on own socks. (24 mos.; Meisels and others 2003, 52) • Pull her shoes off at naptime. (24 mos.; Meisels and others 2003, 52)

References

American Academy of Pediatrics. 2004. *Caring for Your Baby and Young Child: Birth to Age 5.* 4th ed. Edited by S. P. Shelov and R. E. Hannemann. New York: Bantam Books.

Apfel, N. H., and S. Provence. 2001. *Manual for the Infant-Toddler and Family Instrument (ITFI).* Baltimore, MD: Paul H. Brookes Publishing.

Baillargeon, R. 2004. "Infants' Physical World," *Current Directions in Psychological Science* 13 (3): 89–94.

Bard, K., and C. Russell. 1999. "Evolutionary Foundations of Imitation: Social-Cognitive and Developmental Aspects of Imitative Processes in Non-Human Primates." In *Imitation in Infancy: Cambridge Studies in Cognitive and Perceptual Development,* edited by J. Nadel and G. Butterworth. Cambridge, UK: Cambridge University Press.

Barrera, M. E., and Mauer, D. 1981. "The Perception of Facial Expressions by the Three-Month-Old." *Child Development* 52:203–6.

Bauer, P. 2002a. "Early Memory Development." In *Handbook of Cognitive Development,* edited by U. Goswami. Oxford, England: Blackwell.

———. 2002b. "Long-Term Recall Memory: Behavioral and Neuro-Developmental Changes in the First Two Years of Life." *Current Directions in Psychological Science* 11 (4): 137–41.

———. 2004. "Getting Explicit Memory off the Ground: Steps Toward Construction of a Neuro-Developmental Account of Changes in the First Two Years of Life." *Developmental Review* 24:347–73.

———. 2007. "Recall in Infancy: A Neurodevelopmental Account." *Current Directions in Psychological Science* 16 (3): 142–46.

Bauer, P. J., and J. M. Mandler. 1989. "One Thing Follows Another: Effects of Temporal Structure on 1- to 2-Year Olds' Recall of Events." *Developmental Psychology* 8:241–63.

Bayley, N. 2006. *Bayley Scales of Infant and Toddler Development.* 3rd ed. San Antonio, TX: Harcourt Assessment.

Brazelton, T. B. 1992. *Touchpoints: Your Child's Emotional and Behavioral Development.* New York: Perseus Books.

Bronson, M. 2000. *Self-regulation in Early Childhood: Nature and Nurture.* New York: Guilford Press.

Brooks-Gunn, J., and G. Duncan. 1997. "The Effects of Poverty on Children." *The Future of Children* 7 (2): 55–71.

Butterworth, G. 1999. "Neonatal Imitation: Existence, Mechanisms and Motives." In *Imitation in Infancy: Cambridge Studies in Cognitive and Perceptual Development,* edited by J. Nadel and C. Butterworth. New York: Cambridge University Press.

California Department of Education (CDE). 2005. Desired Results Developmental Profile (DRDP). Sacramento, CA: California Department of Education. http://www.cde.ca.gov/sp/cd/ci/desiredresults.asp (accessed February 7, 2007).

Carey, S. 2001. "On the Very Possibility of Discontinuities in Conceptual Development." In *Language, Brain, and Cognitive Development: Essays in Honor of Jacques Mehler,* edited by E. Dupoux. Cambridge, MA: MIT Press.

Clements, D. H. 2004. "Major Themes and Recommendations." In *Engaging Young Children in Mathematics: Standards for Early Childhood Educators,* edited by D. H. Clements and J. Samara. Mahwah, NJ: Lawrence Erlbaum Associates.

Coplan, J. 1993. *Early Language Milestone Scale: Examiner's Manual.* 2nd ed. Austin, TX: Pro-ed.

Engaging Young Children in Mathematics: Standards for Early Childhood Mathematics Education. 2004. Edited by D. H. Clements and J. Sarama. Mahwah, NJ: Lawrence Erlbaum Associates.

Fenson, L., and others. 1976. "The Developmental Progression of Manipulative Play in the First Two Years." *Child Development* 47 (1): 232–36.

Fogel, A. 2001. *Infancy: Infant, Family, and Society.* 4th ed. Belmont, CA: Wadsworth/Thomson Learning.

Fuson, K. C. 1988. *Children's Counting and Concepts of Number.* New York: Springer-Verlag.

Gallistel, C. R., and R. Gelman. 1992. "Preverbal and Verbal Counting and Computation." *Cognition* 44 (1–2): 43–74.

———. 1978. *The Child's Understanding of Number.* Oxford, England: Harvard University Press.

Ginsburg, H. P., and S. Opper. 1988. *Piaget's Theory of Intellectual Development.* 3rd ed. Englewood Cliffs, NJ: Prentice Hall.

Gopnik, A., A. Meltzoff, and P. K. Kuhl. 1999. *The Scientist in the Crib: Minds, Brains, and How Children Learn.* New York: William Morrow.

Gowen, J. W. 1995. "Research in Review: The Early Development of Symbolic Play." *Young Children* 50 (3): 75–84.

Hart, B., and T. R. Risley. 1999. *The Social World of Children: Learning to Talk.* Baltimore, MD: Paul H. Brookes Publishing.

Howe, M., and M. Courage. *1993.* "On Resolving the Enigma of Infantile Amnesia." *Psychological Bulletin* 113 (2): 305–26.

Hulit, L. M., and M. R. Howard. 2006. *Born to Talk: An Introduction to Speech and Language Development.* 4th ed. New York: Pearson Education.

Kail, R. 1990. *The Development of Memory in Children.* 3rd ed. New York: W. H. Freeman.

Lally, J. R., and others. 1995. *Caring for Infants and Toddlers in Groups: Developmentally Appropriate Practice.* Washington, DC: Zero to Three Press.

Legerstee, M. 1997. "Contingency Effects of People and Objects on Subsequent Cognitive Functioning in Three-Month-Old Infants." *Social Development* 6 (3): 307–21.

Lerner, C., and A. L. Dombro. 2000. *Learning and Growing Together: Understanding and Supporting Your Child's Development.* Washington, DC: Zero to Three Press.

Lerner, C., and L. A. Ciervo. 2003. *Healthy Minds: Nurturing Children's Development from 0 to 36 Months.* Washington, DC: Zero to Three Press and American Academy of Pediatrics.

Madole, K., and L. Oakes. 1999. "Making Sense of Infant Categorization: Stable Processes and Changing Representations." *Developmental Review* 19 (2): 263–96.

Mandler, J. M. 2000. "Perceptual and Conceptual Processes in Infancy." *Journal of Cognition and Development* 1 (1): 3–36.

Mandler, J., and L. McDonough. 1993. "Concept Formation in Infancy." *Cognitive Development* 8 (3): 291–318.

———. 1998. "On Developing a Knowledge Base in Infancy." *Developmental Psychology* 34 (6): 1274–88.

Mangione, P. L., J. R. Lally, and S. Signer. 1992. *Discoveries of Infancy: Cognitive Development and Learning.* Sacramento, CA: Far West Laboratory and California Department of Education.

Mareschal, D., and R. French. 2000. "Mechanisms of Categorization in Infancy." *Infancy* 1 (1): 59–76.

Meltzoff, A. N., and M. K. Moore. 1983. "Newborn Infants Imitate Adult Facial Gestures." *Child Development* 54: 702–9.

———. 1989. "Imitation in Newborn Infants: Exploring the Range of Gestures Imitated and the Underlying Mechanisms." *Developmental Psychology* 25 (6): 954–62.

———. 1999. "Persons and Representation: Why Infant Imitation Is Important for Theories of Human Development." In *Imitation in Infancy: Cambridge Studies in Cognitive and Perceptual Development,* edited by J. Nadel and G. Butterworth. New York: Cambridge University Press.

Meisels, S. J., and others. 2003. *The Ounce Scale: Standards for the Developmental Profiles (Birth–42 Months).* New York: Pearson Early Learning.

Mix, K., J. Huttenlocher, and S. Levine. 2002. *Quantitative Development in Infancy and Early Childhood.* New York: Oxford University Press.

Moser, R. F. 1995. "Caregivers' Corner. Fantasy Play in the Sandbox." *Young Children* 51 (1): 83–84.

National Research Council and Institute of Medicine. 2000. *From Neurons to Neighborhoods: The Science of Early Childhood Development.* Committee on Integrating the Science of Early Childhood Development. Edited by J. Shonkoff and D. Phillips. Washington, DC: National Academies Press.

O'Brien, M. 1997. *Meeting Individual and Special Needs: Inclusive Child Care for Infants and Toddlers.* Baltimore, MD: Paul H. Brookes Publishing.

Parks, S. 2004. *Inside HELP: Hawaii Early Learning Profile: Administration and Reference Manual.* Palo Alto, CA: VORT Corporation.

Perry, J. P. May, 2003. "Making Sense of Outdoor Pretend Play." *Young Children* 58 (3): 26–30.

Rogoff, B. 1990. *Apprenticeship in Thinking: Cognitive Development in Social Context*. New York: Oxford University Press.

Rogoff, B., and P. Chavajay. 1995. "What's Become of Research on the Cultural Basis of Cognitive Development?" *American Psychologist* 50 (10): 859–77.

Rogoff, B., and others. 2003. "Firsthand Learning Through Intent Participation." *Annual Review of Psychology* 54:175–203.

Ruff, H., and M. Rothbart. 1996. *Attention in Early Development: Themes and Variations*. New York: Oxford University Press.

Segal, M. 2004. "The Roots and Fruits of Pretending." In *Children's Play: The Roots of Reading*, edited by E. F. Zigler, D. G. Singer, and S. J. Bishop-Josef. Washington, DC: Zero to Three Press.

Siegel, D. J. 1999. *The Developing Mind: How Relationships and the Brain Interact to Shape Who We Are*. New York: Guilford Press.

Starkey, P., and R. G. Cooper. 1980. "Perception of Numbers by Human Infants." *Science* 210 (4473): 1033–35.

Starkey, P., E. S. Spelke, and R. Gelman. 1990. "Numerical Abstraction by Human Infants." *Cognition* 36 (2): 97–128.

Sternberg, R. J., and E. L. Grigorenko. 2004. "Why We Need to Explore Development in Its Cultural Context." *Merrill-Palmer Quarterly* 50 (3): 369–86.

Vygotsky, L. S. 1978. *Mind in Society: The Development of Higher Psychological Processes*. Cambridge, MA: Harvard University Press.

Whitehurst, G., and C. Lonigan. 1998. "Child Development and Emergent Literacy." *Child Development* 69 (3): 848–72.

Wynn, K. 1998. "Numerical Competence in Infants." In *The Development of Mathematical Skills,* edited by C. Donlad. Hove, East Sussex, UK: Psychology Press.

Youngblade, L. M., and J. Dunn. 1995. "Individual Differences in Young Children's Pretend Play with Mother and Sibling: Links to Relationships and Understanding of Other People's Feelings and Beliefs." *Child Development* 66:1472–92.

11-012 PR12-001 9-12 10M

OSP 12 128322